FORTRESS • 79

ISRAELI FORTIFICATIONS

of the October War 1973

SIMON DUNSTAN

ILLUSTRATED BY STEVE NOON

Series editors Marcus Cowper and Nikolai Bogdanovic

First published in Great Britain in 2008 by Osprey Publishing,
Midland House, West Way, Botley, Oxford OX2 0PH, United Kingdom
443 Park Avenue South, New York, NY 10016, USA
Email: info@ospreypublishing.com

ISBN 978 1 84603 361 2

Editorial by Ilios Publishing Ltd (www.iliospublishing.com)
Page layout by Ken Vail Graphic Design, Cambridge, UK (kvgd.com)
Cartography: Map Studio, Romsey, UK
Index by Glyn Sutcliffe
Originated by PDQ Digital Media Solutions
Printed in China through Bookbuilders

08 09 10 11 12   10 9 8 7 6 5 4 3 2 1

A CIP catalogue record for this book is available from the British Library.

FOR A CATALOGUE OF ALL BOOKS PUBLISHED BY OSPREY MILITARY
AND AVIATION PLEASE CONTACT:

NORTH AMERICA
Osprey Direct, c/o Random House Distribution Center, 400 Hahn Road,
Westminster, MD 21157
Email: info@ospreydirect.com

ALL OTHER REGIONS
Osprey Direct, The Book Service Ltd, Distribution Centre,
Colchester Road, Frating Green, Colchester, Essex, CO7 7DW, UK
Email: customerservice@ospreypublishing.com

www.ospreypublishing.com

ACKNOWLEDGEMENTS

Despite repeated requests, neither the Egyptian nor Israeli armed forces
felt able to assist in the preparation of this book. It is a measure as to how
controversial the Bar Lev Line remains. Accordingly the contribution by
Stuart Bracken is all the more important with his extensive archive of
photographs and material. My thanks also to Lon Nordeen for his
enthusiastic assistance in matters relating to aerial combat during the
War of Attrition. Unless otherwise credited all photographs are courtesy
of the Israeli National Photo Archives – with many thanks to Sharon of
the Israeli Government Press Office.

ARTIST'S NOTE

Readers may care to note that the original paintings from which the
colour plates in this book were prepared are available for private sale.
All reproduction copyright whatsoever is retained by the Publishers.
All enquiries should be addressed to:

Steve Noon, 50 Colchester Avenue, Penylan, Cardiff, CF23 9BP, UK

The Publishers regret that they can enter into no correspondence upon
this matter.

THE FORTRESS STUDY GROUP (FSG)

The object of the FSG is to advance the education of the public in the
study of all aspects of fortifications and their armaments, especially
works constructed to mount or resist artillery. The FSG holds an annual
conference in September over a long weekend with visits and evening
lectures, an annual tour abroad lasting about eight days, and an annual
Members' Day.

The FSG journal FORT is published annually, and its newsletter Casemate
is published three times a year. Membership is international. For further
details, please contact:

The Secretary, c/o 6 Lanark Place, London W9 1BS, UK

Website: www.fsgfort.com

THE WOODLAND TRUST

Osprey Publishing are supporting the Woodland Trust, the UK's leading
woodland conservation charity, by funding the dedication of trees.

CONTENTS

ISRAELI FORTIFICATIONS OF THE OCTOBER WAR 1973

'If you entrench yourself behind strong fortifications, you compel the enemy to seek a solution elsewhere.'

Karl von Clausewitz, *On War*

ONLY LET THERE BE PEACE

The Six Day War of June 1967 was possibly the most stunning victory in the annals of modern military history. Only a week previously, many Israelis believed their country to be on the eve of destruction on a par with the Holocaust. Surrounded by a hostile Arab world, Israel faced invasion from the armies of four separate nations. Yet within six hours, the Israeli Air Force (IAF) destroyed the military and political will of these implacable enemies. Within six days, the Israel Defense Forces (IDF) comprehensively destroyed their armed forces and changed the political complexion of the Middle East to this day. Before the war there was a rueful Israeli saying that went: 'Israel is like a sausage – easy to carve up.' In an overwhelming triumph of arms, the Israelis increased their landmass by a factor of four and achieved militarily defensible borders for the first time since the creation of the state in 1948. In the euphoria of victory, Israeli confidence knew no bounds and a new saying was heard in the cafés of Tel Aviv and the newly captured city of Jerusalem: 'Damascus is just an hour away, Cairo perhaps two.'

The combination of Israeli air power and armoured might was the key to victory in the Six Day War. In the words of the war correspondent Randolph S. Churchill: 'a feat of arms unparalleled in all modern history'. Neither the Arabs nor the Israelis were able to find any political accommodation following the conflict leading to renewed hostilities and the creation of extensive field fortifications along Israel's vastly expanded borders.

Vital terrain was gained on the West Bank of the Jordan River, the Golan Heights and the Sinai Peninsula. Yet these greatly extended borders now had to be defended against an Arab world that would not countenance any form of political or territorial compromise except an immediate return to the borders ante-bellum. The prospect of lasting peace seemed as elusive as ever. The defence of the occupied territories was now a pressing reality. The strategic depth afforded by the Sinai Peninsula demanded its total retention but with the minimum of forces given Israel's chronic shortage of manpower as compared to her Arab neighbours. Similarly the Golan Heights was vital ground to be held at all costs. The dilemma was how to achieve these aims with the least expenditure of men and resources. Fortunately, the rugged terrain on both the Golan Plateau and the Sinai Peninsula favoured the defenders, since both were predominately mountainous with few roads to aid any attacker. The only feasible avenue of attack was across the Suez Canal, yet the waterway itself presented a formidable obstacle that would have to be surmounted first before any assault could be successful. The Israelis had no intention of allowing this to happen. The outcome was the War of Attrition. With the resumption of hostilities in July 1967, the fortification of the IDF positions along the Suez Canal became necessary to reduce casualties. This led to the construction of the fabled Bar Lev Line. It was just one element in an increasingly sophisticated defence strategy that had all the hallmarks of a complex three-dimensional chess game, albeit a contest that frequently resulted in the deaths of soldiers and airmen in the ever-shifting sands of the Sinai Desert and of sailors in the waters that defined the Sinai Peninsula. To extend the chess analogy further, the static Bar Lev Line represented the line of pawns on the board of battle. Behind them, the artillery acted as rooks capable of rapid linear movement along the front and providing heavy firepower at every point of contact. The Israeli Armored Corps (IAC) provided the bishops, capable of rapid movement and shock action

Victory in the Six Day War brought the IDF to the banks of the Suez Canal where troops dug in, such as this machine-gun team with their .30-cal. M1919 Browning as a Sikorsky S-58 helicopter comes in to land. Such basic positions provided scant protection against Egyptian artillery fire and as the casualties rose the Sikorsky S-58 helicopters were widely used in the medical evacuation role. First acquired in February 1958, the Sikorsky S-58 helicopter equipped IAF No. 124 Squadron 'Rolling Sword' and 28 were in service at the outbreak of the Six Day War when they acted in the search and rescue (SAR) role for downed pilots, air assault of Israeli paratroopers, tactical airlift and for aeromedical evacuation missions. By 1969, the S-58 had been superseded by the Bell 205 in the SAR role.

The first field fortifications along the Suez Canal were rudimentary and comprised little more than a sandbagged weapons pit and an underground bunker beneath. Both were vulnerable to a direct hit from artillery fire. Of particular interest, this soldier has an M16 rifle suggesting that he is a paratrooper since this weapon was a rare commodity in the IDF in the late 1960s. It was policy to replace reservist troops stationed on the Bar Lev Line with seasoned regulars such as paratroopers during times of tension or impending conflict. However, this was not to be in October 1973.

at any place of enemy incursion or in support of the pawns on the Bar Lev Line. With their ability to attack from unexpected directions, the Special Forces in their helicopters or frogmen's Zodiacs were the knights, striking swiftly and without warning deep inside enemy territory. The queen on this particular battlefield was undoubtedly the IAF. Highly trained and motivated, the IAF was Israel's most potent strike force and the guardian of the skies over Israel. At the outset of the War of Attrition that was fought from July 1967 until August 1970, the IAF was employed for combat air defence and tactical close air support against an increasingly sophisticated Egyptian missile air defence system. In a testament to its professionalism, the IAF made the complex transition from a French inventory of aircraft to an American one during a conflict, with the newfound capacity to undertake strategic bombing deep in the hinterland of Egypt. In a bitter, protracted war, both sides fought to the point of exhaustion.

Throughout the war the Bar Lev Line had proved its worth in reducing the casualty rate of Israeli front-line troops. Following the War of Attrition, it was repaired and strengthened. The sand rampart was heightened to 18m and was extended along the length of the waterway. Another line of fortifications and sand barriers was created further inland to protect artillery and infantry formations lying in support of the Bar Lev Line. The network of roads and supply depots was extended to allow them enhanced mobility across the harsh terrain. But as the weeks of ceasefire turned into months, the Bar Lev Line diminished in importance within the IDF high command as they were now fighting a new enemy of fedayeen inside the occupied territories and terrorists across Europe, exemplified by the Munich massacre at the Olympic Games of 1972. For three years all was quiet on the Egyptian front, during which time several fortifications were shut down along the Suez Canal and others were allowed to fall into a state of disrepair. With economic prosperity growing in Israel, complacency grew in the political and military establishment. On the holiest day in the Jewish religious calendar, the fortifications of the Bar Lev Line along the Suez Canal and the Purple Line on the Golan Heights were put to the ultimate test. On Yom Kippur, 6 October 1973, the armies of both Egypt and Syria attacked the state of Israel simultaneously.

CHRONOLOGY

5–11 June 1967	The Third Arab-Israeli War, commonly known as the Six Day War, results in a spectacular Israeli victory and the occupation of much Arab territory.
June 1967 to September 1968	Known to the Egyptians as 'The Period of Defiance and Persistence'.
1 July 1967	Egyptian incursion across Suez Canal at Ras al Ush.
21 October 1967	Egyptian naval forces sink the Israeli destroyer INS *Eilat* killing 47.
15 June 1968	The War of Attrition begins, with sparse Egyptian artillery bombardment of the Israeli front line on the east bank of the Suez Canal.
September 1968 to March 1969	Known to the Egyptians as 'The Period of Active Defence'.
30 October 1968	Israeli commandos attack targets deep in Egypt causing Nasser to cease hostilities for a few months while fortifications around hundreds of important targets are built. Simultaneously, Israel begins construction of the Bar Lev Line.
March 1969 to August 1970	Known to the Egyptians as 'The Period of Attrition'.
3 March 1969	Nasser officially rescinds the ceasefire of June 1967.
8 March 1969	Egyptian artillery and air force begins massive bombardment of the Bar Lev Line resulting in Israeli casualties. The IDF retaliates with deep raids into Egyptian territory, causing severe damage.
20 July 1969	Almost the entire IAF attacks Egyptian positions in the northern Canal sector. The aerial offensive continues until December and degrades the Egyptian air defence system significantly. It reduces the intensity of the artillery bombardment against the Bar Lev Line but shelling with lighter weapons, particularly mortars, continues.

17 October 1969	The USA and USSR begin diplomatic talks to end the conflict.
9 December 1969	The Rogers Plan is publicized. It calls for Egyptian 'commitment to peace' in exchange for the Israeli withdrawal from the Sinai. Both countries reject the plan.
22 January 1970	President Nasser secretly flies to Moscow to acquire more modern weapons including a new air defence system manned by Soviet troops.
15 March 1970	The first fully operational Soviet SAM site in Egypt is completed. It is part of three air defence brigades that the USSR sends to Egypt.
30 June 1970	Following the Soviets' direct intervention, known as Operation *Kavkaz*, Washington fears an escalation and redoubles efforts toward a peaceful resolution to the conflict.
7 August 1970	A ceasefire agreement is reached, forbidding either side from changing 'the military status quo within zones extending 50km to the east and west of the ceasefire line'. Soon after the ceasefire, Egypt begins moving SAM batteries into the zone even though the agreement explicitly forbids new military installations. By October, there are approximately 100 SAM sites in the zone.
28 September 1970	President Nasser dies of a heart attack, and his Vice President, Anwar al-Sadat takes over. Sadat agrees to end the War of Attrition and almost immediately begins planning for the next conflict which would take place three years later in October 1973: a period of 'No War, No Peace'.
6 October 1973	Egypt and Syria attack Israel simultaneously achieving considerable initial success. Within days the Bar Lev Line has fallen.

BUILDING THE LINE

Despite the totality of the Arab defeat in the Six Day War and the formal ceasefire that ensued, hostilities hardly stopped along the banks of the Suez Canal. Skirmishes were commonplace as Egyptian troops made night-time incursions into the Sinai Desert and Egyptian artillery periodically fired on Israeli positions along the waterline. At the outset these were rudimentary comprising a couple of half-tracks and a sandbagged weapons pit. The first Israeli fatality to hostile action following the war was recorded on 15 June 1967. At this time, a single armoured brigade reinforced with additional infantry held the Suez front. On 19 June 1967, the Israeli Cabinet met to discuss the aftermath of the war and voted for the evacuation of almost the entire Sinai Peninsula and the Golan Heights on the understanding that both would be demilitarized and with two further fundamental conditions. These

were the freedom of passage by sea and air through the Straits of Tiran into the Red Sea and no further attempts by the Syrians to divert the sources of the Jordan River, both of which were the principal *casus belli* of the conflict. However the West Bank and the Holy City of Jerusalem were deemed to be vital to Israeli security and indeed part of Eretz Yisrael, or the real Israel of biblical precedence to include both Judea and Samaria. In the event, the Cabinet decision was academic in face of the resolution passed at the Arab League conference in Khartoum on 29 August 1967 when the delegates declared a policy of 'No recognition. No negotiations. No peace.' towards the state of Israel. Meanwhile the people of Israel were euphoric following their complete triumph on the battlefields at a cost of fewer than 800 deaths. Accordingly, no party in government could now readily consider forsaking the fruits of victory as had happened in 1956 under the pressure of world opinion. Instead the United Nations promulgated the ambiguous Resolution No. 242 that satisfied none of the warring parties although Israel and Jordan reluctantly agreed to its provisions: Egypt and Syria did not. The stage was set for renewed hostilities.

Following the Six Day War, many Egyptian commanders were summarily sacked for their incompetence. The new Chief of Staff of the Armed Forces was General Abdul Moniem Riadh while General Mohammed Fawzy became the new War Minister. On 1 July 1967, Lieutenant-General Ahmed Ismail Ali was appointed to command the remnants of the Egyptian field army on the Suez Canal. On the same day the Egyptian Army launched a raid across the Suez Canal in support of their forces holding Port Fuad at the northern end of the canal and the ground to the south bordering an area of extensive salt marshes that was unsuitable for Israeli armour. The raiders took up positions in the village of Ras el Ush, approximately 12km south of Port Fuad. An Israeli armoured force from Kantara mounted an assault against the entrenched Egyptians but after an inconclusive encounter lasting several hours with casualties incurred by both sides, the Israelis withdrew. Although

An IDF M38A1 Jeep speeds through the ruins of Al Kantara during a patrol on 10 July 1969. Such patrols in softskin vehicles were highly vulnerable to ambushes by Egyptian infiltrators or mines that were laid in profusion to inflict a constant trickle of Israeli casualties during the War of Attrition.

The oil installations and refineries of Suez City go up in flames following an IDF bombardment on 24 October 1967 in retaliation for the sinking of the INS *Eilat* three days before. At bottom left of the photograph is Port Tewfiq and the southern entrance to the Suez Canal. Following such attacks, the city's civilian population was evacuated. Thereafter, the whole of Suez City came under the guns of Taoz Tzeider while Maoz Masreq was built just opposite to Port Tewfiq.

barely mentioned in Israeli accounts, Ras el Ush became a rallying call to the Egyptian armed forces as the beginning of the 'Period of Defiance' against the IDF. Over the following days artillery duels across the canal caused further casualties. On 8 July 1967, the situation escalated when two Israeli fighter-bombers attacked Egyptian artillery emplacements and tank positions on the west bank of the canal. The Egyptians responded immediately with a fierce artillery bombardment of Israeli positions in Kantara followed by an air attack by the remnants of the Egyptian air force on 14 July: an event that caught the Israelis totally by surprise.

As the fighting escalated on the banks of the canal, a political conflict erupted when General Dayan suggested through the offices of the UN that the Suez Canal should be reopened to traffic of all parties and the royalties shared between Egypt and Israel. Although the Egyptians were keen to reopen the canal, they could not contemplate sharing any revenue with the Israelis and threatened to fire on any Israeli vessel that navigated the waterway. When the Israelis put that threat to the test, the craft was promptly blown apart by artillery fire. The Suez Canal was to remain closed to all shipping until the spring of 1975. Since the Six Day War, the Israeli Navy had been tasked with patrolling the additional 650km of coastline of the Sinai Peninsula with just three destroyers, the INS *Eilat, Haifa* and *Jaffa*. On the night of 11/12 July 1967, the flagship of the Israeli Navy, the INS *Eilat* (formerly HMS *Zealous*), was patrolling the Mediterranean coastline together with two motor torpedo boats when they encountered two Egyptian P-6 torpedo boats off Romani. The latter were engaged and sunk by gunfire during a 30-minute battle. The Egyptians soon gained their revenge. On the evening of 21 October 1967, the INS *Eilat* was on patrol once more but as she passed Port Said she was struck towards the stern and soon after amidships by SS-N-2 Styx surface-to-surface missiles fired from a pair of Soviet-supplied Komar (Mosquito) Class missile boats. As desperate efforts were made to save the sinking ship, the *Eilat* was struck by another Styx missile approximately 90 minutes after the first attack. Of the crew of 199, 47 were killed and a further 41 injured.

To the Egyptians, the battle of Ras el Ush and the sinking of the INS *Eilat* as well as the air attack of 14 July 1967 did much to assuage the humiliation of the Six Day War as each of the services within the Egyptian armed forces had acquitted themselves well. These events still resonate to this day in Egyptian military history – see www.mmc.gov.eg/History/gg3.htm. In early September, Minister for War General Mohammed Fawzy announced that a new phase in the undeclared hostilities termed the 'Active Deterrent' had begun as masses of Soviet military material arrived to re-equip the Egyptian armed forces. On 8 September, the Egyptian Army unleashed a massive bombardment on Kantara and the sector northwards. For several hours, 150 artillery batteries fired some 10,000 shells against IDF positions. Despite the onslaught, the Israelis suffered surprisingly few casualties with ten dead and 18 wounded; many of them caught in the open while playing football. Even so such losses were a severe shock to the IDF and the high command allocated more funds to fortify the rudimentary canal defences. The Southern Command was tasked with drawing up plans to implement further protection for the troops. However, little had been achieved before 26 October 1967 when another massive Egyptian artillery barrage engulfed the entire length of the front-line defences for over nine hours. A further 15 soldiers were killed with 34 wounded.

The IDF retaliated by bombarding the oil refineries at Suez as well as the towns of Ismailia and Suez, as they had after the sinking of INS *Eilat*. The Egyptian President, Colonel Gamal Abdel Nasser, firmly indicated his resolve by evacuating some 400,000 civilians from the Canal Zone and made no attempt to rebuild the refineries so as to pre-empt further Israeli attacks. With only limited artillery assets and the opposing towns just empty shells, the IDF turned to other means to retaliate. On the night of 31 October 1967, a helicopter-borne commando force under the redoubtable paratrooper Colonel Dani Matt demolished a bridge at Kina deep inside Lower Egypt and an electrical transmission station at Naj Hamadi as well as damaging a dam and cutting a high-voltage power line between Cairo and the Aswan Dam causing

The Aerospatiale SA 321K Super Frelon was the first heavy lift helicopter to enter service with the IAF under the name of Tzir'a or Hornet. Twelve Tzir'a were acquired from April 1966 and they equipped IAF No. 114 Squadron. During the Six Day War they were employed extensively for medical evacuation missions, the insertion of assault troops and the transport of equipment to the front lines. However it was during the War of Attrition that the Tzir'a won lasting fame as the principal means to insert Special Forces troops during the many commando raids into Egyptian territory such as Operations *Tarnegol-53* to capture an Egyptian P-12 radar system and *Rodus* against Shadwan Island, an Egyptian stronghold in the Gulf of Suez. The Tzir'a saw action in both the Yom Kippur War and during Operation *Peace for Galilee* in 1982, and the helicopter continued to serve as a VIP transport until it was withdrawn from service in 1991.

Soon after the Six Day War, various Palestinian factions began to foment unrest in the occupied territories administered by Israel particularly in the West Bank areas of Judea and Samaria with numerous terrorist attacks by armed insurgents from secure bases in Jordan and southern Lebanon. Between 1967 and 1970, some 5,840 incidents were recorded along the Jordanian border. In the meantime, international terrorism became widespread with passenger airliners being hijacked on a regular basis as a bargaining ploy to release captured terrorists or to publicize the Palestinian cause. Such heinous acts culminated in the killing of 11 Israeli athletes at the Munich Olympics of 1972. These incidents did much to distract the Israeli Government from the rising threats posed by Syria and Egypt on the Golan Heights and Suez Canal respectively where the IDF's military defences were being dangerously neglected. Here, men of the Magav Border Police patrol along a track in November 1968 checking for mines accompanied by an M38A1 Jeep and a Walid APC captured from the Egyptian Army in the Six Day War.

widespread blackouts in the capital. The attack was undertaken some 700km inside Egypt and the raiders returned without incurring any casualties. The raid gave President Nasser grave cause for concern as to the vulnerability of the Egyptian hinterland. Over the next five months a lull ensued along the Suez Canal while a local militia was raised inside Egypt to counter further raids. Nevertheless, desultory artillery and sniper fire continued to plague the Israeli troops in their front-line positions.

The lull in the fighting allowed the Israelis the opportunity to construct more formidable field fortifications along the Suez Canal. Nevertheless, a fierce debate continued to rage within the higher echelons of the IDF high command as how to address the deteriorating situation along the Suez Canal. From the time of the creation of the state of Israel, the received military doctrine in time of war with any neighbouring Arab country was to take the fighting to the enemy's territory as quickly as possible since the landmass of Israel proper was so small. At its narrowest, Israel was just 15km wide with the coastal town of Netanya within range of Jordanian artillery. Similarly, the northern settlements and towns around the Sea of Galilee were dominated by Syrian guns and subject to repeated artillery barrages over the years. On the southern flank, Israel and the Negev Desert remained vulnerable to Egyptian attack along the wide-open border. The campaigns of 1956 and 1967 had proved conclusively the efficacy of an offensive doctrine based on the superiority of the IDF in armoured warfare and the devastating use of airpower against its Arab neighbours.

The overwhelming victory in June 1967 now gave Israel the priceless prize of defence in depth. No longer were the northern kibbutzim and the beaches of Netanya within range of Syrian or Jordanian guns but there was to be no lasting peace. With the Khartoum declaration of the 'Three No's', Israel was now obliged to defend its greatly expanded borders. While previously the IDF operated on short internal lines of communication that allowed the rapid redeployment of forces from one front to the next, it now had to transport every bullet, shell and tomato a further 240km to the Canal Zone at considerable extra cost in vehicles and manpower. Similarly many more resident troops were needed to defend the vast expanse of the Sinai Peninsula while the Navy had five times the amount of coastline to patrol and the IAF a four-fold expanded area of responsibility to maintain air superiority. This entailed a far greater use of equipment but both the Navy and IAF were now severely compromised by the French arms embargo instituted by General de Gaulle prior to the Six Day War. In many ways victory had been achieved through the employment of French jet aircraft but now the supply of spare parts and airframes had been halted.

Defence equipment procurement was now a high priority for the IDF, both to replace planes and tanks lost during the war and to overcome the French arms embargo. Fortunately the Six Day War had had a profound effect on American public opinion and by extension the US Government. Bogged down in an increasingly costly and protracted war in Vietnam, the consummate military victory achieved in just six days was met with widespread admiration. The notion of Israel as a biblical David fighting the Goliath of the Arab world was a potent image to the American people. Israel was now seen as a bastion of democracy in a region of autocratic rulers supplied with Soviet weapons who were therefore subject to the evil influence of communism. The Middle East became another cockpit of superpower rivalry. Furthermore, President Lyndon Baines Johnson was a staunch supporter of Israel. Accordingly the arsenal of democracy was now opened to the IDF. Significant numbers of A-4 Skyhawk fighter-bombers were supplied to the IAF soon after the war, followed by the formidable F-4 Phantom II; the first of which arrived in September 1969. Similarly significant numbers of M48 and M60 Patton tanks were provided to Israel. New self-propelled guns were required for the artillery branch while the infantry demanded new armoured personnel carriers (APCs) to replace the ancient fleet of World War II half-tracks. There was just not enough money to meet every requirement. For a military establishment imbued with a successful doctrine of the offensive, the notion of devoting scant resources to building static field fortifications along the Suez Canal and across the Golan Heights was anathema.

The dichotomy in the IDF high command remained unresolved. There were two principal schools of thought. One school headed by Major-General Israel Tal, the commander of the IAC, together with Major-General Ariel Sharon, GOC Training, advocated the concept of '*egrofei shiryon*' or 'mailed fists' whereby armoured formations were held deep in the Sinai Desert well beyond Egyptian artillery and rocket range but ready to mount devastating counteroffensives against any enemy incursion at short notice. The Suez Canal itself would be patrolled by light mobile units with just a handful of observation posts along the waterway itself. By these means, the IDF would be able to utilize the terrain and the strategic depth of the Sinai Desert to the full while capitalising upon the IDF's proven superiority in manoeuvre warfare. The other school remained convinced that the IDF must preserve a credible presence along the canal and lakes so as to discourage any Egyptian incursion at the water line. Again armoured formations were to be stationed inland ready to mount a counteroffensive against an Egyptian attack supported by the full weight of the IAF.

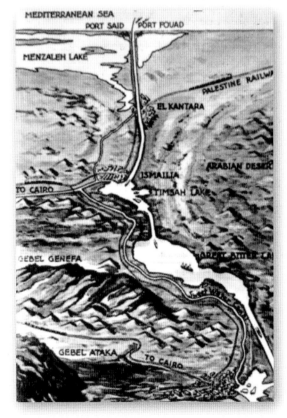

This 1920s postcard depicts the main geographical and topographical features of the Suez Canal Zone with the man-made canal linking the Mediterranean Sea with Lake Timsah, the Great and Little Bitter Lakes and on to the Gulf of Suez at Port Tewfiq. The *Maozim* of the Bar Lev Line were mainly situated along the man-made sections of the Suez Canal. With remarkable prescience, the French engineer, Ferdinand de Lesseps, who created the Suez Canal predicted at the opening ceremony in November 1869 that he had marked the site of a future battlefield. (Author)

The IDF Chief of Staff, Lieutenant-General Haim Bar Lev, headed the second school. His reasoning was largely political, since it was deemed essential that the Egyptians be prevented from mounting a limited offensive and establishing a lodgement on the eastern bank of the Suez Canal whereupon they would attempt to make it permanent by seeking a UN Security Council resolution for an immediate ceasefire. It was also essential to provide increased protection to any troops on the front line: while many families might just accept the deaths of their sons and daughters in a war when the survival of the nation was at stake, it was quite another matter to have their sons blown to pieces by artillery fire whilst playing football in times of supposed peace. In his capacity as Chief of Staff, General Bar Lev had the ear of government. Accordingly his views prevailed and the decision was taken to create a line of fixed fortifications along the Suez Canal and the Bitter Lakes from the Mediterranean to the Red Sea, a distance of some 180km.

The task of developing the new defence line of strongpoints was entrusted to Major-General Avraham 'Bren' Adan, a highly experienced armour officer and the creator of the Sinai Division after the Six Day War. General Bar Lev ordered him to create a team drawn from all branches and services of the IDF as part of an overall reassessment of the defence plans for the Sinai Peninsula. Improved field fortifications were already under consideration following a study by Major-General Yeshayahu Gavish, GOC Southern Command, that suggested strongpoints opposite those sectors where the main roads in Egypt led to the canal, namely at Kantara, Ismailia, the Firdan Bridge, Deversoir and Suez City, as well as commanding the roads on the eastern bank of the canal leading to the vital Mitla and Gidi passes that were the principal access points back to Israel. The plan was predicated on the assumption that the IAF would firstly neutralize the Egyptian air defence system thus assuring air superiority before providing close air support to the ground troops in the role of 'flying artillery' given the deficiencies of the army's artillery branch. The operational plan for the defence of the Sinai Peninsula was codenamed *Shovach Yonim* or *Dovecote*. While the Sinai Division comprised three regular armoured brigades as a standing force, there was usually a fourth armoured brigade of reservists training in the Sinai Desert. In times of tension, this unit could be called upon to support the regular formation and provide a credible deterrent against any limited Egyptian incursion that might result in a politically unacceptable lodgement on the eastern bank of the Suez Canal. It was also intended that in times of tension the troops in the strongpoints along the canal – usually reservists – would be replaced by regulars or paratroopers whose level of training was considered to be higher.

In the classic 'two up and one in reserve' formation, two of the armoured brigades would be deployed forward to protect the 180km-long canal line with one brigade in reserve. The forward brigades were responsible for the protection of the strongpoints in their sector. Those strongpoints that were in difficult terrain or more than 20 minutes distant from the main supply route that ran parallel to the canal were to have an attached tank platoon of three tanks for their immediate

Major-General Avraham 'Bren' Adan was tasked with devising the first plans for what became known as the Bar Lev Line. His concept for the field fortifications along the Suez Canal embraced traditional defence works as well as modern electronic monitoring devices combined with rapid reaction armoured forces stationed close to the waterway. General Adan subsequently became the commander of the IAC in 1972. During the October War of 1973 he commanded the 252nd Armored Division in the desperate defence of the Sinai Peninsula before leading the Israeli counteroffensive across the canal.

support. This supply route was commonly some 10km from the canal and was known as the Artillery Road, since it also allowed artillery units to deploy rapidly along the length of the front. In each brigade sector, two armoured battalions, each of three tank companies, were stationed close to the road so they too could deploy rapidly to block any crossing attempts. These companies were expected to reach the canal or any threatened strongpoint in under 30 minutes. The third armoured battalion was held in reserve close to the Lateral Road that also ran parallel to the canal but at a distance of some 30km. This unit was expected to reach the canal within two hours of an alert order. The plan called for the fourth or reserve armoured brigade, if present in the Sinai, to concentrate at Tassa on the Central Road so that it would be able to support any sector under threat.

Nevertheless, *Dovecote* was predicated on the assumption that prior to the outbreak of general warfare there would be sufficient warning time to mobilize the reserves. However, the new borders created by the Six Day War had changed the dynamics of the IDF's offensive doctrine. The strategic depth now afforded by the Sinai Desert, so longed for by the IDF high command since the War of Independence, allowed them the option to either launch a pre-emptive strike if war seemed imminent – although with all the serious international political disadvantages that would accrue – or to allow the enemy the first strike and thereafter use the expanse of the Sinai Desert to employ the Israeli predominance in manoeuvre warfare to the full: a choice denied to them prior to June 1967 when the enemy was lying so close to Israeli population centres. With the Sinai in Israeli possession, the warning time against enemy aircraft attack increased from four minutes to 16, a crucial difference of a further 240km of flying time. But by creating static fortifications along the Suez Canal, the bulk of the Egyptian Army permanently stationed on the western bank was just 150m from the Israeli front-line troops. This allowed the Egyptians to change from a defensive to offensive posture in the shortest possible time and thus any warning time was potentially negated to a dangerous and unacceptable degree. There is a considerable difference between 240km and 150m. Accordingly, more troops were needed close to the canal to provide support to any line of strongpoints.

With its parachute brake deployed, an F-4E of IAF No. 201 Squadron 'Ha'ahat' lands after a mission during the War of Attrition. The first four Israeli McDonnell Douglas F-4E Phantom II fighter-bombers landed at Hazor AFB on 5 September 1969 and entered service with IAF No. 201 Squadron 'Ha'ahat' or 'The One'. The Kurnass or Sledgehammer, as the Phantom was known in Israeli service, conducted its first operational sortie just one month later on 5 October and its first attack mission during Operation *Pirkha* on 22 October, destroying an SA-2 site near Abu Suweir. Thereafter, the Kurnass multi-role combat aircraft gave the IAF a strategic strike capability that was employed extensively during the War of Attrition to engage targets deep inside Egypt as well as in the Suez Canal Zone. Eight Kurnass fighter-bombers were lost during the War of Attrition with six to AAA and SAMs and one to a Syrian MiG-21 while the other was destroyed in an operational accident in March 1970.

THE BAR LEV LINE

As an armour officer, General Adan was a keen advocate of a flexible defence that relied on a strong armoured force to mount rapid counterattacks at any point of incursion. His difficult task was to reconcile this with the requirement for a fixed linear defence along the canal itself to prevent the possibility of an Egyptian lodgement on the eastern bank. Within short order, General Adan's team devised a comprehensive plan for the new field fortifications to be integrated with the bulk of the armoured forces deployed in the rear – the concept of *Shovach Yonim*. The plan called for some 20 fortifications that were to act only for early warning and self-defence against artillery and small unit infantry attack. These were to be sited and constructed to give a maximum degree of visual observation while exposing a minimum number of troops to enemy artillery fire: the need to reduce casualties remained paramount. As the canal was dead straight for much of its length, it was possible to observe to a distance of five kilometres in any direction. Accordingly, the observation posts were to be positioned at intervals of every 10km. At night, observation was to depend on an electronic warning system that tripped an alarm if enemy intruders broke the beam projected along the length of the waterline. In the event, the technology did not fulfil the requirement at the outset so night-time patrolling was necessary instead.

Each position was to have some 15 to 20 troops that could be augmented with more manpower in times of tension; in theory 30 men under the command of a field officer. Typically 75 per cent of the men would be combat infantrymen and the remainder administrative staff. Each defensive position comprised an area from as compact as 50 by 50m made of four interconnected firing posts with one at each corner of the compound to much larger complexes. Close by was an enclosed bunker for the weapons' crews as protection against artillery fire. All the posts were connected by deep trenches, often with overhead cover of hessian material, to disguise movement and provide some much-needed shade against the sun, or curved armoured covers to provide protection against air-burst weapons. At the centre of the

One of the most important tasks for the soldiers of the Bar Lev Line was the continuous assessment of Egyptian troop dispositions and defence works on the west bank of the Suez Canal to forestall any incursion across the waterway. Observation towers and optical periscopes were in constant use as were the first generation of night observation devices for 24-hour surveillance. The War of Attrition was also notable for the first use of UAVs, or unmanned aerial vehicles, carrying reconnaissance cameras in combat.

compound was a command bunker with strong overhead cover capable of resisting the heaviest calibre artillery weapons and most aerial bombs. In tiers beside the command bunker were the medical aid station, sleeping quarters and the mess hall. Separate latrines and showers were also provided. Each fortification had sufficient ammunition, food, water and medical supplies to enable the strongpoints to resist for several days if need be. Buried telephone wires as back-up communications augmented the radio links to headquarters.

During the 11 years it took to construct the Suez Canal, the spoil from the excavation was heaped along the eastern bank. Over the years this grew in height as more sand and mud from continual dredging of the canal was deposited on top. The strongpoints were built into and on top of this bank of solidified sand and mud, with further sand barriers around the positions to minimize enemy observation and protect against direct-fire weapons. In some positions, ramps were incorporated into the structure to allow attached tanks to be stationed so as to provide enfilade fire along the length of the waterway. Further tank firing positions were created in the sand rampart between the field fortifications to allow direct fire to be brought to bear against Egyptian positions on the opposite bank of the canal. Each fortified position had a parking area for vehicles, usually adjacent to the main gate, which was concealed from the enemy and where supply trucks could be unloaded and patrol vehicles kept and serviced if necessary. Extensive minefields and barbed-wire entanglements encircled each position to discourage ground attack and enemy infiltration.

In December 1968, General Adan submitted his plan to General Gavish as GOC Southern Command. The latter reiterated his requirement for more strongpoints in sensitive areas he had identified. When the plan was discussed at GHQ, the concept of combining the principles of a fixed and mobile defence was accepted by all those present, including generals Tal and Sharon although the latter suggested that the strongpoints on the canal be much smaller with only a couple of observers with infantry in bunkers further back from the waterline. In the event, the overall plan was approved with the Chief of Staff, General Bar Lev, adding a few more strongpoints at the northern and southern ends of the Canal Zone. In all, 31 field fortifications were to be built along the Suez Canal, Lake Timsah, the Bitter Lakes, the Gulf of Suez and on the Mediterranean Sea (see map on p. 27). Drawing on his experiences as a youth when he supervised the fortification of small isolated settlements in the Negev Desert during the War of Independence, General Adan called the strongpoints *Maoz* – the Hebrew word for a keep or the strongest structure in a castle.

Construction began immediately under the direction of the Israeli Engineering Corps employing thousands of soldiers, civilians and combat engineers and much of the plant equipment that Israel possessed. Work continued on a 24-hour basis. The design of the fortifications was kept as simple as possible to reduce costs with a layered system of overhead protection incorporating tiers of reinforced concrete blocks and steel railway ties for strength. The command bunkers and living accommodation were prefabricated and made from curved steel panels for maximum rigidity and strength; the whole structure being encased in rock gabions many metres thick in order to defeat artillery shells and direct fire weapons. In some areas such as potential crossing points, a cluster of fortifications was built with a principal position and several subsidiary observation posts. Progress was rapid due largely to the lull in the artillery bombardments of the Egyptian army. Completion of the strongpoints was scheduled for 15 March 1969.

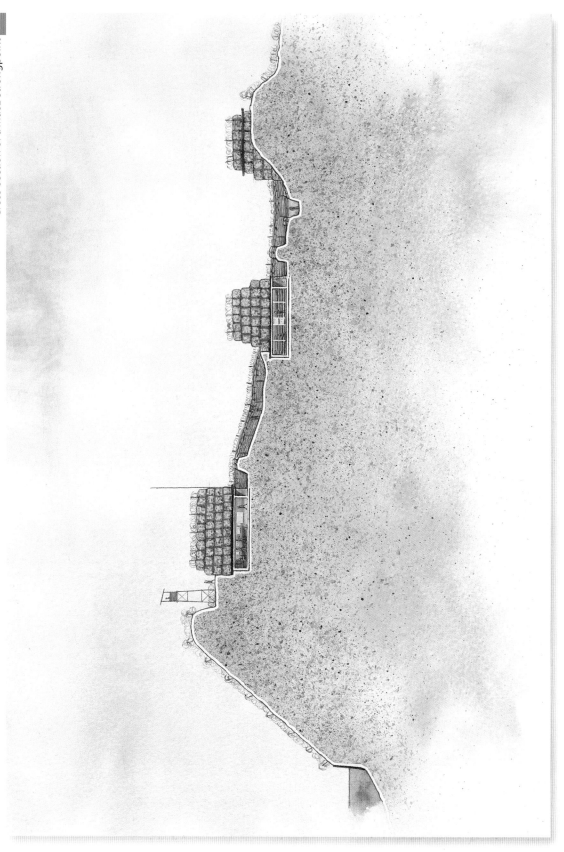

However, the *Maozim* were just one element in General Adan's comprehensive revision of *Dovecote*. Along the waterline itself, the sand barrier was raised to a height of five to 10m and shaped at an angle of 45 degrees from the surface of the canal so as to impede any type of armoured fighting vehicle. The face of the sand barrier was studded with anti-personnel mines and barbed-wire entanglements to discourage fighting patrols. Patrol roads were constructed running parallel to the canal just behind the fortifications. These were paved to reduce the risks from mines planted by infiltrating Egyptian patrols. Supply roads to and from the fortifications were laid and linked up with the principal north–south road that lay some 10km inland. It was now paved along its length and widened to provide two-way traffic with numerous pre-registered artillery firing points immediately adjacent to the road. It also allowed tanks and artillery pieces to move rapidly along the length of the front. For this reason it became known as Artillery Road. It ran behind a ridge of sand hills that provided an important vantage point overlooking the canal and formed a vital defence line in time of war. A second north–south road was similarly upgraded that lay some 30km inland. Known as the Lateral Road, it linked the major supply bases of Tassa and Baluza that supported the forward field fortifications and reserve forces in time of war. It also acted as the main conduit to move large armoured formations from one sector to another while being beyond the range of Egyptian artillery. Between the Artillery and Lateral roads were a network or roads, running predominantly from east to west, underground headquarters, water storage facilities, communications bunkers, observation posts, stores depots and repair shops: indeed the whole panoply of an army in residence with the principal headquarters of Southern Command at Refidim, formerly Bir Gifgafa, in the middle of the Sinai Desert. Refidim also acted as the forward IAF base in the Sinai together with those at Etam, Etzion and Ras Nas Rani (later Ophir) on the Red Sea as well as Sharm el-Sheik as a naval base.

THE WAR OF ATTRITION

For good or ill, the field fortifications along the Suez Canal became known in the Israeli national press as the 'Bar Lev Line'. It was named after General Haim Bar Lev, the incumbent Chief of Staff of the IDF. In the mind's eye of the general public, it conjured up comparisons with the Maginot and Siegfried lines of World War II while the Suez Canal was perceived as the 'world's largest and longest anti-tank ditch'. Unfortunately the IDF did little to disabuse the

This detail view of a *Maoz* field fortification shows the standard form of construction with the exterior comprised of numerous rock gabions encased in wire mesh and the roof improvised from railway ties taken from the Palestine Railway that used to run from Cairo via El Kantara to El Arish and on to Palestine. It was built by the British during World War I. The rock-filled gabions had to be transported from quarries deep in the Sinai Peninsula. (Stuart Bracken)

Israeli people of this notion, as it remained primarily a political rather than military statement of intent. It was one the Egyptians were willing to put to the test in no uncertain terms. At the very time that the IDF high command decided on the construction of the Bar Lev Line, President Nasser had decided to go to war with Israel in order to recover the lost lands of the Sinai Peninsula. Nevertheless, after several months of concerted debate, during which the IDF was able to construct much of the Bar Lev Line, the Egyptian military and political leadership were now in accord as to their strategy.

In the inspiring rhetoric beloved of the Arab world, the timeframe from the Six Day War of June 1967 through August 1968 was now formally declared as 'The Period of Defiance'; the time from September 1968 through February 1969 was 'The Period of Active Defence' and the new strategy to be unveiled was to be Al-Istinaf: 'The Period of Attrition'. As espoused by General Riadh, Chief of the General Staff, the objectives were as follows:

1. To destroy the fortifications of the Bar Lev Line.
2. To prevent the Israelis from reconstruction of the fortifications once they were destroyed.
3. To make life intolerable for the Israeli forces along the Suez Canal and inflict as many casualties as possible.
4. To inspire an offensive spirit in Egyptian troops.
5. To refine and practise canal-crossing operations.

These objectives were based on careful analysis of the relative strengths and weaknesses of both the Egyptian and Israeli forces. General Riadh realized that the Egyptian armed forces lacked an effective command and control system, due largely to the complete lack of political direction and the extraordinary autonomy and unprofessionalism displayed by some senior officers: prior to the Six Day War many were more concerned with the running of lucrative sporting clubs in Cairo than the profession of arms. In addition, both the Air Force and the Navy acted as independent organizations with no concerted control at all. These problems were rigorously addressed with many more senior appointments being made on merit rather than patronage. The integration of command structures embracing the Army, Navy and Air Force proceeded apace. A new Air Defence Command was created in July 1968 to coordinate all anti-aircraft artillery (AAA) and surface-to-air missile (SAM) units in order to blunt the superiority of the IAF.

In October 1967, General Riadh was given an affirmation of the Egyptians' ability to employ sophisticated weapon systems when the INS *Eilat* was sunk by Styx anti-ship missiles on his birthday. While the weaknesses of the Egyptian armed forces were addressed, the Egyptian high command identified the areas of Israeli dominance as their superiority in air combat and in manoeuvre warfare. The former was to be countered by the expansion of SAM units equipped with the SA-75 Dvina system, commonly know by its NATO designation as the SA-2 Guideline, and the latter by the massive employment of Soviet anti-tank weapons such as the Ruchnoy Protivotankovy Granatomyot, or RPG rocket-propelled grenade, and the 9M14 Malyutka (NATO codename AT-3 Sagger). The intention was to saturate any Israeli armoured offensive by a mass of missiles and RPGs while main battle tanks and self-propelled guns acted as direct-fire support weapons behind the infantry screen.

An M50 155mm self-propelled howitzer undertakes a fire mission during the War of Attrition. Artillery was the principal weapon employed by the Egyptian Army during the protracted conflict using a wide array of Soviet ordnance. On many occasions forward observation teams were infiltrated into the Sinai Peninsula to provide accurate target information to the waiting guns that caused a debilitating rate of IDF casualties, with black-edged photographs of fallen soldiers appearing with appalling regularity in Israeli newspapers. Starved of modern weapon systems, the IDF artillery branch was hard pressed to counter the profligate number of Egyptian artillery pieces and mortars employed during the War of Attrition.

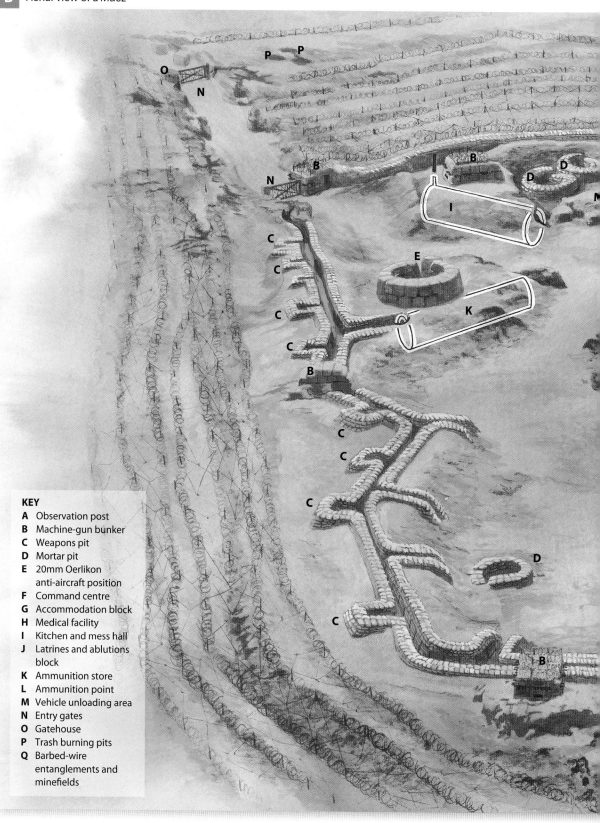

KEY

A Observation post
B Machine-gun bunker
C Weapons pit
D Mortar pit
E 20mm Oerlikon anti-aircraft position
F Command centre
G Accommodation block
H Medical facility
I Kitchen and mess hall
J Latrines and ablutions block
K Ammunition store
L Ammunition point
M Vehicle unloading area
N Entry gates
O Gatehouse
P Trash burning pits
Q Barbed-wire entanglements and minefields

SUEZ CANAL

The Bar Lev Line was named after the contemporary Chief of Staff of the IDF (1968–71), Lieutenant-General Haim Bar Lev, shown here during the Yom Kippur War when he assumed overall control of Southern Command after the failure of its GOC, Major-General Shmuel Gonen, in the opening days of the war. General Bar Lev confers on the telephone in the IDF war room deep underground in the bowels of the Kiryah in Tel Aviv on 19 October 1973 with the situation map behind him showing the expanding IDF bridgehead across the Suez Canal and the impending breakout southwards to encircle the Egyptian Third Army.

Furthermore, the Egyptian armed forces now enjoyed an absolute majority in numbers of AFVs and artillery pieces, as well as a massive preponderance of manpower. The creation of the Bar Lev Line and its tacit admission of a static linear defence played into the hands of Egyptian material superiority. High Israeli casualties along the Suez Canal would have a debilitating effect on Israeli public opinion, while mobilizing the reserves to counter a protracted Egyptian offensive would significantly damage the Israeli economy. Politically, the Egyptians saw the line as an attempt to ensure the continuation of the military status quo and the definition of the Suez Canal as the de facto border between Israel and Egypt. This was utterly unacceptable. On 3 March 1969, President Nasser announced that the ceasefire agreement of June 1967 with Israel was null and void. Five days later, the Egyptians launched a massive bombardment along the Suez Canal that was to last almost 80 days without ceasing. The War of Attrition was resumed in earnest.

Boredom was a constant enemy to the troops stationed on the Bar Lev Line so anyone with musical skills was always a welcome addition to any unit, such as these soldiers relaxing in their sleeping and living quarters at Maoz Milano. These tubular steel structures were immensely strong but also claustrophobically cramped with hardly room to stand upright.

Women have always been an integral part of the IDF and they perform many important support roles. Here, a corporal telephonist named Fanny hangs out her washing on the Bar Lev Line or more exactly at the Southern Command headquarters complex at Refidim that controlled all the *Maozim*.

Day after day artillery shells impacted on the newly constructed fortifications. None were penetrated or put out of action although some suffered serious damage. The armoured reserves were able to advance to their firing ramps and engage the Egyptian positions according to plan. The self-propelled artillery units were able to roam the front in response to the fire direction from the observation posts along the canal while the IAF maintained air superiority over the battlefield. The Navy continued to dominate the extensive coastline of the Sinai Peninsula against Egyptian incursion. Casualties were light and mainly among the exposed crews of the artillery weapons. The concept of the Bar Lev Line seemed to be working, although some strongpoints were incomplete when hostilities were renewed leaving significant stretches without observation.

THE PURPLE LINE

Arguably, the IDF victory on the Golan Heights in the closing hours of the Six Day War was of greater significance than that in the Sinai Peninsula. The towns and villages near the Sea of Galilee below the Golan escarpment were now safe from Syrian artillery fire while the vital head waters of the Jordan River were in Israeli hands: as was the dominating feature of Mount Hermon

C FOLLOWING PAGE: MACHINE-GUN BUNKER

Fundamental to the construction of the Bar Lev Line was the widespread use of prefabricated components that were made in Israel and transported to the Suez Canal. A typical machine-gun emplacement comprised a steel shell with integral firing slits. Steel railway ties usually in two layers protected the roof of the shell. These supported a layer of interlocking concrete blocks above which were rock gabions as the final level of protection against artillery fire. All sides of the steel shell were lined with the standard concrete blocks that had lifting holes in their sides and four holes through the top and bottom faces. Through these were slotted steel 'rebar' (reinforcing bars) to strengthen the whole structure. The outsides were then lined with yet more rock gabions. Another prefabricated item was the concrete funnel that was aligned with the firing slits of the weapons. An emplacement commonly had up to three firing slits but the number used was dependent on the terrain and the fields of fire covered by the position. This method of construction was typical for many weapons emplacements and other structures such as observation posts.

The Southern Front in the Yom Kippur War

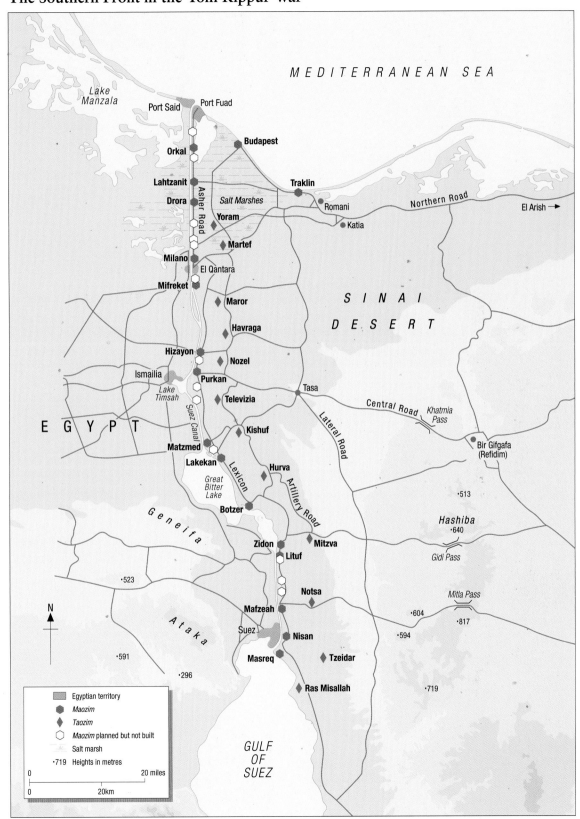

MEDITERRANEAN SEA

Lake Manzala

Port Said · Port Fuad

Budapest

Orkal

Lahtzanit

Traklin

Drora

Salt Marshes · Romani

Yoram

Northern Road

Katia

El Arish →

Martef

Asher Road

Milano

El Qantara

Mifreket

Maror

S I N A I

D E S E R T

Havraga

Hizayon

Nozel

Ismailia

Purkan

Tasa

Lake Timsah

Televizia

Central Road · Khatmia Pass

Suez Canal

Kishuf

Matzmed

Bir Gifgafa (Refidim)

Lakekan

Hurva

E G Y P T

Lexicon

Great Bitter Lake

Botzer

·513

Artillery Road

Lateral Road

Hashiba

·640

Zidon · Mitzva

G e n e i f a

Lituf

Gidi Pass

·523

Notsa

Mitla Pass

N

Mafzeah

·604 ·817

A t a k a

Suez

Nisan

·594

·591

Masreq · Tzeidar

·296

Ras Misallah

·719

GULF OF SUEZ

	Egyptian territory
	Maozim
	Taozim
	Maozim planned but not built
	Salt marsh
·719	Heights in metres

0 ——————— 20 miles

0 ——————— 20km

that allowed observation deep into Syrian territory. Over 2,000m above sea level, Mount Hermon was of immense strategic value to the Israelis and a heavily fortified observation post, bristling with electronic monitoring and optical viewing devices, was quickly established on its heights. On the Golan Plateau itself, the Israelis built numerous pillboxes and blockhouses, 112 in all, as well as 17 fortified positions just to the west of the ceasefire line with the Syrians. Running north to south for some 65km, it was known as the Purple Line from its colour on the maps of UNTSO personnel. The United Nations Truce Supervisory Organisation (UNTSO) had the unenviable task of monitoring the ceasefire and trying to maintain order between the two antagonistic belligerents.

Unlike in the Sinai Desert, there was no room to trade space for time to allow the reserves to be mobilized as the Golan Plateau occupied by the Israelis was just 27km wide east to west. The volcanic plateau is undulating ground comprising basalt rock and lava flows that is extremely punishing to the suspension of any vehicle. It is poor tank country except in the south where the area is more suitable to cultivation. Because of the broken ground, there are just five roads running from east to west with only one major one, the age-old Damascus Road that ran from the Syrian capital to the Mediterranean port of Haifa. Similarly, there are only two significant roads running north to south with one following parallel to the path of the Purple Line from Rafid in the south to Masada while the other runs diagonally across the plateau beside the Trans-Arabian Pipeline or TAP that carries oil underground from Saudi Arabia via Jordan to Lebanon and the Mediterranean Sea. Nevertheless, the Israeli defence plan of the Golan Plateau was based on the mobility of its armoured forces manoeuvring behind the line of static fortifications. As one Israeli commander on the Golan stated:

> With the exception of the bunkers and village defensive positions, the entire Israeli defensive force was capable of movement. Tanks, self-propelled artillery, infantry and armoured infantry were all in motion or could be at short notice. Artillery batteries moved set-up, fired, rested, moved and fired again within minutes of receiving an order ... the entire firepower of the Israeli battle force could move from one fulcrum to another in an infinite variety of combinations. An attacker could never be certain just what combination he might encounter. It was a strategy based on mobility and the paramount Israeli requirement that the expense in men and equipment be minimal.

To this end, the Israelis built numerous tracks across the plateau to allow the deployment of tanks and supply vehicles across the difficult terrain as well as tracks to the 17 'fortified tactical localities' along and behind the Purple Line. These were perched on some of the numerous volcanic mounds that dotted the plateau like gigantic anthills. Known as 'tels' or mounts, they offered excellent observation over the Purple Line and across the Damascus Plain, with wide fields of fire from the interlocking bunkers and firing pits. Other higher promontories to the west such as Tel Faris, Tel Hermonit and Tel Avital sprouted with sophisticated electronic monitoring and observation devices with communications equipment to coordinate rapidly the defensive fire plans of the artillery and the close air support of the air force. The bunkers were well protected against artillery fire by extensive overhead cover and thick walls of wire wrapped gabions of basalt rock. Each one was held by up to an infantry platoon but customarily between 12 and 15 troops when

tension was low. The infantry were armed with multiple automatic and anti-tank weapons. Dense wire entanglements and minefields protected the positions. Nearby were elevated firing ramps to allow a platoon of tanks to engage enemy targets at maximum range. Forward of the line of bunkers and running the length of the Purple Line was a formidable anti-tank ditch some five metres deep with the spoil heaped up on the Syrian side to a height of some three metres. Along its length, the ditch was bordered by dense minefields, both anti-personnel and anti-tank, that were laid so as to channel enemy armour into killing zones dominated by the tanks on their ramps. With the command headquarters at Nafekh, the Golan Plateau was normally defended by two resident regular brigades, the 1st 'Golani' Infantry Brigade and the 188th 'Barak' Armored Brigade.

HOLDING THE LINE

On the southern front, the War of Attrition continued unabated. In March 1969, there were some 84 firing incidents rising to 475 in April. Although much damage was inflicted, most of the positions along the Bar Lev Line survived the incessant bombardment. The Egyptians now mounted repeated commando raids across the canal striking at individual fortifications as well as mobile patrols, supply convoys and rear installations. Inevitably, Israeli casualties rose: in March seven killed and 29 wounded; in April 21 killed and

A Mirage IIICJ of IAF No. 119 Squadron 'Atalef' (Bat) stands ready for flight in May 1973 adorned with eight kill markings, denoting Mirage 58 as one of the greatest MiG killers during the War of Attrition. The Mirage or Shahak (meaning Firmament) was the air-superiority fighter par excellence during the fierce battles above the Bar Lev Line. With their superior aerial gunnery training, Mirage pilots fully exploited the delta-wing configuration of their aircraft at low levels where guns were commonly used at ranges of 50 to 100m and air-to-air missiles from 700 to 3,000m. During the War of Attrition, the Mirage IIICJ was credited with destroying approximately 100 enemy aircraft in aerial combat.

D **FOLLOWING PAGE: AFV REVETMENTS**

A fundamental aspect of the Bar Lev Line was the use of mobile forces stationed deeper in the Sinai Desert to come to the aid of the strongpoints along the Suez Canal. This support was commonly in the form of main battle tanks and self-propelled artillery as well as ground attack aircraft of the IAF. To create defence in depth, the IDF constructed numerous prepared firing positions for both tanks and self-propelled guns. These hull-down positions were simple scrapes in the ground with stone-lined sides and a concrete base. The latter provided a level firing platform that is especially important for artillery pieces to allow them to undertake precise pre-registered fire plans. Since they were dug into the ground, these positions

gave protection to the vulnerable suspension and tracks of the vehicles against artillery fire while some positions, such as the one illustrated with an M109 155mm self-propelled howitzer, had a fully enclosed concrete housing to provide further protection against enemy fire or indeed the elements. Prepared hull-down scrapes were built close to and between the *Maozim* so that tanks could be rapidly deployed to the waterline to counter any crossing of the canal. Further hull-down scrapes, known as 'fins' were built some 1,500 to 1,800m behind the waterline to counter AFVs on the huge sand ramparts, known as the 'Pyramids', constructed by the Egyptians on the opposite side of the canal that overlooked the *Maozim*.

The Purple Line

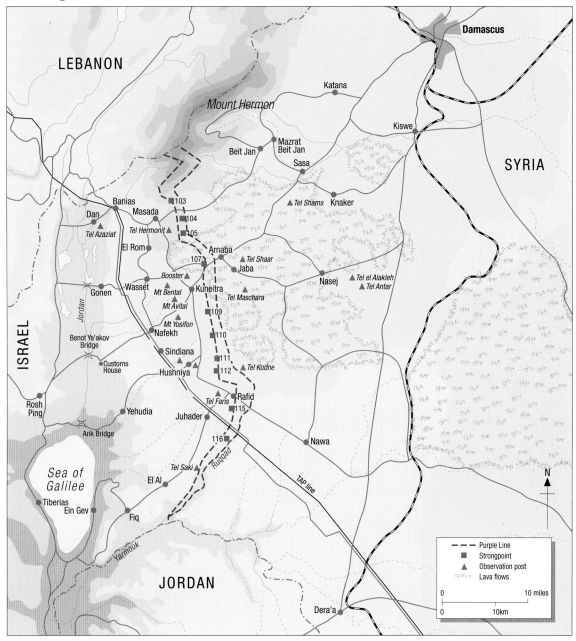

34 wounded. Some fortifications were cut off for days because of the intense artillery fire and, on occasions, the wounded had to wait for many hours before medical evacuation. The Israeli response was to mount more deep strike commando raids. On 28 April 1969, the Special Forces struck again at the same dam and bridge at Naj Hamadi and destroyed high-tension power lines to Lower Egypt. Meanwhile the IAF maintained air superiority over the Sinai with five air-to-air kills in April and May without encroaching significantly into Egyptian airspace.

The rising casualty rate was causing considerable concern to the Israeli high command. Some senior officers called for a more offensive posture beyond the tactic of limited commando raids. The IAF now enticed the Egyptians into a series of dogfights over the Gulf of Suez and increasingly deeper inside Egyptian airspace. Ten MiG-21s were lost by 7 July 1969, and on the following day Israeli Mirages shot down seven Syrian MiG-21s. Nevertheless, the successes in the air had little impact on the ground where Egyptian artillery continued to pound the fortifications of the Bar Lev Line. On the night of 10 July 1969, Egyptian commandos crossed the Suez Canal in assault boats and mounted a highly successful raid against an Israeli tank leaguer near the Maoz Masreq opposite Port Tewfiq in which seven Israeli soldiers were killed, five wounded and others taken prisoner. In the same week, the former commander of the IAF, General Ezer Weizman, visited the Bar Lev Line and quickly learned the ordeal of the infantry when he received 'the shelling of my life – a hell of fire'. He made his views plain to the cabinet Defense Committee meeting held on 16 July 1969. The committee proposed a major air campaign employing the full resources of the IAF against the Egyptian defences along the Suez Canal and further inland as necessary, since the many Special Forces raids did not seem to deter the continuing Egyptian artillery barrages. Between March and August the total of Israeli casualties was 75 dead and 195 wounded.

On 20 July 1969, the full might of the IAF was unleashed against the northern canal defences in Operation *Boxer*. With the world's attention on Neil Armstrong's first steps on the moon, 159 tons of bombs and 72 napalm canisters were dropped on Egyptian positions causing hundreds of casualties. Four days later, the IAF hit SAM and AAA sites on the central and southern sectors of the canal destroying many sites as well as artillery emplacements. This reduced the level of fire against Israeli fortifications but led to a rise in small arms and mortar attacks. In August, they rose to a daily average of 16.6 incidents with 13 Israeli dead and 55 wounded over the month. And so the cycle of violence continued with renewed Israeli air attacks and commando raids leading to heavy Egyptian casualties and the occasional lull in the hostilities until they began again with renewed artillery bombardments and their own commando raids along the canal.

In order to speed installation under the guns of the Egyptians, most of the defence works of the Bar Lev Line were prefabricated in Israel and transported to the Suez Canal Zone. This was the standard machine-gun pit capable of taking the .30-cal. M1919 and .50-cal. M2 Browning machine guns. Note the slots for ammunition stowage in this weapons pit that remains at Maoz Masreq, which was known to the Egyptians as The Quay. (Stuart Bracken)

In the last five months of 1969, there was a monthly average of 512 incidents of enemy fire resulting in 65 Israeli dead and 180 wounded giving a total of 140 dead and 375 wounded since the War of Attrition resumed in March, with 45 per cent of the total casualties caused by artillery fire. This indicated only a marginal reduction in the casualty rate since the IAF was employed in force against the Egyptian defences and artillery emplacements although the upward trend in casualties was halted. Mines laid by infiltrators damaged many patrol vehicles and supply trucks with a steady stream of casualties. Moreover, the Egyptians continued to mount numerous raids against the Bar Lev Line including a concerted attack against one *Maoz* on 29 November 1969. They also mounted a daring underwater raid against the port of Eilat on the night of 15 November 1969, sinking two Israeli boats. The War of Attrition was achieving its purpose, as, despite ongoing diplomatic efforts by the superpowers to achieve a ceasefire, Egypt showed no inkling of halting the hostilities along the Bar Lev Line. Her demands remained constant and implacable: the withdrawal of the Israelis from the Sinai Peninsula.

In a significant escalation of the conflict, the Israeli government decided to unleash the IAF in deep penetration raids into Egypt in a strategic bombing campaign using its newly acquired combat aircraft in the form of the McDonnell-Douglas F-4E Phantom II while the role of ground attack was undertaken by the A-4E and A-4H Skyhawk, known in Israeli service as the Ahit or Vulture. On 22 October 1969, the Phantom made its combat debut with the IAF in an attack against an SA-75 battery at Abu Sueir while on 4 November a pair of Phantoms flew low over Cairo creating sonic booms to remind the inhabitants of their vulnerability to Israeli airpower. It was not without reason that the Israelis christened their Phantom fighter-bombers the Kurnass, or Sledgehammer. The campaign of deep penetration raids began on 7 January 1970 against a host of targets including supply depots, training ce...... and military headquarters buildings; many of them within a 40km radius of Cairo in order to have the maximum effect on Egyptian public opinion, since the press was rigorously controlled and the general public knew little about the War of Attrition along the Suez Canal.

In the same month, President Nasser flew to Moscow to seek medical treatment for his ailing heart and for a new comprehensive air defence system. Embarrassed by the failure of their previous system based on the SA-2 Guideline, the Soviets acted promptly to re-equip the Egyptian armed forces with more modern air defence weapons, including the S-125 Pechora, codenamed SA-3 Goa by NATO, that had a low- and medium-level capability to complement the high altitude coverage of the SA-75MK system, which in turn was superseded by the more effective S-75 Desna and 13D missile. Other up-to-date weapons included the man-portable, shoulder-launched 9K32 Strela-2 or Arrow (NATO codename SA-7 Grail) and the highly mobile, radar-guided ZSU-23-4 self-propelled anti-aircraft gun known as the Shilka. Together these weapon systems posed a serious threat to the IAF, all the more so because many of them were now crewed by Soviet personnel. The pendulum now swung away from the Israelis. On 20 March 1970, Minister of Defense General Moshe Dayan appeared on television and gave a sombre

A lieutenant and a sergeant sitting in a comfortable chair monitor radio traffic in a command bunker of a *Maoz* on the Bar Lev Line in November 1969 while diplomatic talks to end the War of Attrition continue between the USA and USSR. This culminated in the Rogers Plan of 9 December 1969 that called for an Egyptian 'commitment to peace' in exchange for an Israeli withdrawal from the Sinai Peninsula. Both countries rejected the plan and the war continued for the 'moles' of the IDF.

The weapon of choice for the defence of the *Maozim* and *Taozim* against ground attack was the .50-cal. Browning M2HB on account of its reliability in the harsh conditions of the Canal Zone and its anti-material capability against assault boats, amphibious AFVs et al. This twin .50-cal. with gunshield is a former naval mounting salvaged from Israeli naval destroyers as they were phased out of service. Note the prefabricated machine-gun pits in the background that gave protection to the crew and provided ready ammunition for the weapon. This gun pit still exists at Taoz Tzeider with the Gulf of Suez on the horizon. (Stuart Bracken)

OPPOSITE

As the War of Attrition progressed, the Egyptian air defence system became increasingly extensive and sophisticated as new equipments were introduced such as the S-125 Pechora (SA-3 Goa). These were supplied from January 1970 with Operation *Kavkaz* (Caucasus) when Soviet troops of the '11th Dnepropetrovsk' were assigned to man the S-125 batteries. This is the combination of the S-125 Pechora and the SNR-125 (Low Blow) fire-control radar that provided low to medium altitude air defence to complement the high altitude coverage of the SA-75 Dvina. During the War of Attrition, the SAM batteries undertook 124 engagements firing 266 missiles and claiming 32 Israeli aircraft destroyed while the IAF admitted to the loss of 13 aircraft to both SAMs and AAA during the same period. (Lon Nordeen)

address warning of the dangers of the 'Sovietization of the conflict'. On 13 April 1970, Israel suspended its deep penetration raids into Egypt for fear of provoking the Soviet Union further, although a botched bombing raid that killed 47 Egyptian children and wounded 30 others in an elementary school in the village of Bahr El-Bakr was a contributory factor.

The aerial campaign had failed in its aims. It had not ended the unremitting War of Attrition along the Suez Canal where Israeli casualties were still averaging 12 deaths a month. Between October 1969 and March 1970, the IDF suffered 59 killed and 159 wounded on the Sinai Desert/Suez Canal front. In the same time frame, there were 2,427 incidents along the Bar Lev Line, comprising 1,124 with small arms, including snipers, 577 with mortars, 641 with artillery as well as 95 others including air and ground attacks. From March onwards, the number of incidents increased, as did the severity of the artillery bombardments, resulting in yet more Israeli casualties. More worrying was the direct intervention of Soviet troops into the conflict, which greatly complicated Israel's political and military position. The risks of the conflict escalating further were now too dangerous for all parties. At midday on 8 August 1970, a ceasefire sponsored by the United States and supported by the Soviet Union was agreed and the fighting spluttered to an end. IDF Captain David Halevy recalled: 'The quiet along the canal was deafening for anyone who had been there when the artillery was in full blast. Some of the men played chess; others were in the open cleaning rifles or writing letters. In one fort they opened two bottles of wine supplied by the chaplain and drank a I'chayim [to life].'

The agreement stipulated that there was to be no military activity in a 50km-wide zone on each bank of the Suez Canal. Within days the Egyptians began to move missile batteries closer to the Suez Canal. The Israelis protested and some advocated a resumption of hostilities but the Mirage, Skyhawk and Phantom pilots that had borne the brunt of the air campaign were exhausted. Moreover the Israeli people drew a collective sigh of relief at the prospect of peace. Between March 1970 and the ceasefire, Israeli casualties on the Egyptian front amounted to 92 killed and 249 wounded with the death toll rising to almost 20 a month. The black-bordered

photographs of the fallen appearing in the newspapers seemingly every day were a constant reminder of the price being paid by the IDF. The war had cost over 500 dead and 2,000 wounded on all fronts, more than twice the number suffered in the 1956 Sinai campaign. From 15 June 1967 to 8 August 1970, 367 Israeli soldiers were killed on the Egyptian front with 260 of them between March 1969 and August 1970.

In the last five months of the war, the incidence of artillery barrages against the Bar Lev Line rose from 50 to 85 per cent of all incidences by fire that caused considerable damage to the fortifications.

Despite the conditions of the ceasefire, the Israelis began immediate repairs to the line. The Egyptians claimed it was this violation of the ceasefire agreement that prompted them to move forward their SAM batteries. Israeli aircraft losses in the final weeks of the war were becoming unacceptable against the enhanced missile screen that now extended its reach over the Suez Canal. But the lesson was soon forgotten and the belief arose that it was the IAF that had protected the Bar Lev Line and forced a ceasefire on the Egyptians. Similarly, a belief grew that the *Maozim* had more than proved their worth and could hold out against any Egyptian incursion, despite the fact that their artillery had been pulverizing the positions to the end. The Israeli political establishment believed that the war had been won since the status quo had been preserved in the Sinai Peninsula and this belief was

Taoz Tzeider was at the southern end of the Bar Lev Line comprising massive fortified emplacements encasing six French Obusier de 155mm Modele 50 howitzers that dominated Suez City and the southern entrance of the Suez Canal. Today the position is largely intact and forms part of a museum. (Stuart Bracken)

Throughout the War of Attrition in the Sinai Peninsula, unconventional warfare was waged in the occupied territories as various terrorist organizations took up arms against the Israelis, particularly in the West Bank and the Gaza Strip. The latter area was a hotbed of disaffected factions vying for power and influence among the dispossessed inhabitants. Repeated raids were conducted into Israel by the Palestine Liberation Organisation and its numerous offshoots that increasingly absorbed IDF resources as they were obliged to conduct a costly counter-terrorism campaign. Terrorist activity reached its peak in Gaza during 1970. There were 445 security incidents during the year in which 16 Israelis and 45 Arabs were killed. As the Gaza Strip came under the responsibility of Southern Command, its GOC during this period, Major-General Ariel Sharon, devoted more and more of his time and energy to this thorn in the side to the detriment of the Bar Lev Line once hostilities with Egypt ceased in August 1970. Thereafter, resources were diverted from the *Maozim*, many of which were closed and sealed under mounds of sand. Here, IDF soldiers search for weapons and terrorists in a Gaza Strip refugee camp during April 1972.

relayed to the general public. Accordingly there was no real desire to seek a political solution to the problem of the occupied lands. Indeed the war had demonstrated the value of strategic depth in the Sinai Peninsula and the Suez Canal remained as the 'largest and longest anti-tank ditch in the world'.

President Nasser had failed in his aim of forcing the Israelis and the superpowers to reach a political solution to the future of the Sinai Peninsula. He remained resolved to regain the lost territory by any means at his disposal. At last there seemed to be an instrument to blunt the power of the IAF in the ever-expanding missile screen with its modern SAM weapons systems. Egyptian losses had been heavy in material and casualties with estimates as high as 10,000 military and civilians dead. Nevertheless, unlike 1948, 1956 and 1967, the Egyptian armed forces had not been defeated. There emerged a more confident and accomplished officer class and this extended to the rank and file. As Lieutenant-General Abdul Gamasy, Director of Operations during the Yom Kippur War, observed the War of Attrition had been 'a tremendous burden on both Egypt and Israel, … and in the final analysis it was beneficial to Egypt and proved harmful to Israel'. There were those in Israel that agreed. As a former commander of the IAF, General Ezer Weizman, stated that it was the first time since 1948 that the IDF had failed to achieve its military aims: 'It is no more than foolishness to claim that we won the War of Attrition. On the contrary, for all their casualties it was the Egyptians who got the best of it … We, with our hands, smoothed Israel's path to the Yom Kippur War.'

LIFE ON THE LINE

'Seventeen, this is five. Need your sitrep immediately. Over.' 'Five, seventeen here. Busy now. Will send it soonest. Over.' 'Roger that. Over.' 'Only let there be peace. Out.' This was a typical radio exchange between an Israeli headquarters in the Sinai Desert and a *Maoz* officer on the Suez Canal under attack from Egyptian artillery during the War of Attrition. The radio sign-off became a catch phrase and radio calls to and from the outposts on the canal customarily ended with the words: 'Yehi Shalom' or 'Only let there be peace.' The hopes and aspirations in the aftermath of the Six Day War for a lasting settlement between the Arabs and the Israelis were extinguished in the massive weight of artillery fire on Israeli positions in the Sinai Desert that prompted the IDF into the construction of solid field fortifications along the Suez Canal and Bitter Lakes.

Life on the Bar Lev Line and similarly in the bunkers along the Purple Line was arduous and often hazardous. Besides the threat of enemy artillery and mortar fire, there was the constant menace of snipers concealed across the canal, often in the 18m-high eucalyptus and palm trees that flourished along the more fertile western bank of the Suez Canal. Known to Israeli soldiers as 'monkeys', every move in the open had to be measured against the possibility of sniper fire. While artillery barrages were debilitating, not to say terrifying, Israeli soldiers soon learnt that they were virtually immune to harm when sheltering in the fortifications of a *Maoz*. It was the lonely walk to the ablutions or latrine when the individual was at the whim of a casually fired mortar bomb or artillery shell despatched at random to disrupt the daily life of the *Maozim* defenders that inflicted many casualties. Many reservists arrived at the Bar Lev Line for their tour of duty burdened with fishing rods and sun tan lotion in the fond belief they would spend their days fishing in the Suez Canal while topping up their tans. The reality was the oppressive searing heat, often over 50 degrees centigrade; the stench of sweat and fear, of rank boots and socks left out to air and rotting fish in the canal killed by high explosives; the constant curse of flies that invaded every orifice and contaminated all foodstuffs as did the ever shifting windblown sand; the smell of cordite and the concussion of exploding ordnance during a bombardment; the lack of exercise or diversion when under fire and the appallingly cramped living conditions with men crammed into close proximity with each other in the claustrophobic bunkers contaminated by cigarette smoke.

An Israeli soldier tries his luck at fishing on 22 May 1968, just prior to the outbreak of the War of Attrition on 15 June. Of interest, in the background are two moored freighters suggesting that this is the Great Bitter Lake. During the Six Day War, 14 ships were negotiating the Suez Canal and afterwards were trapped by its closure. In the spring of 1975, the Suez Canal was eventually reopened as an international waterway. On 24 May 1975, the German ship MS *Münsterland* docked at Hamburg after a voyage from Australia lasting eight years, three months and five days.

This photograph gives a vivid impression of the cramped conditions of a bunker on the Bar Lev Line as troops cluster in their sleeping accommodation with their faces etched with apprehension as if under artillery bombardment. In fact they are listening to a lecture intended to keep them occupied during the long hours underground. As one soldier sardonically recalled: 'If I had listened to all the lectures properly, I could have achieved a college diploma.'

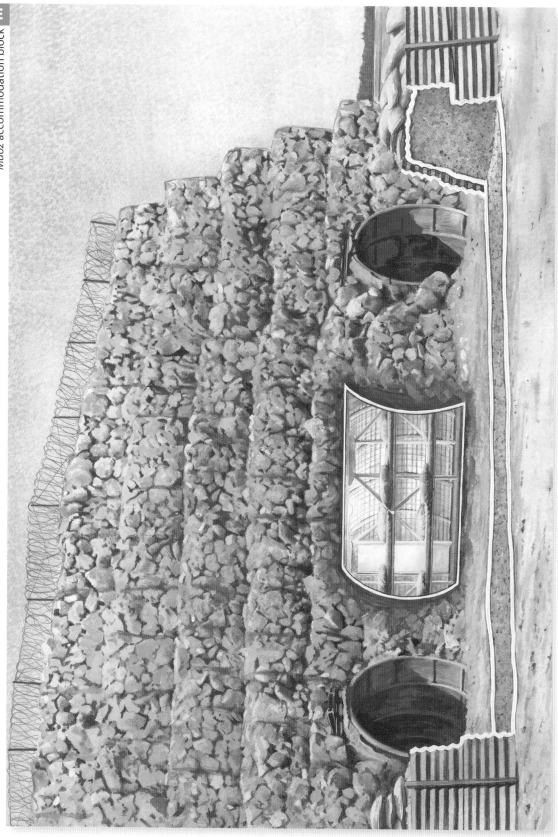

E *MAOZ* ACCOMMODATION BLOCK

The various underground bunkers comprised standardized steel sections that formed a circular tube with the interior strengthened by tubular steel reinforcing supports. These tubular bunkers were configured for various purposes such as command centre, accommodation block, mess hall or ammunition magazine. This plate shows an accommodation block with tiers of bunk beds. The entrance was protected by steel doors with the outside shielded by blast walls against artillery fire. Since this position is close to the banks of the Suez Canal and therefore exposed to direct-fire weapons as well as artillery rounds and aerial bombs, thick layers of rock gabions protect it. This ancient method of field fortification was made up of rocks quarried inland: much of the Sinai mountainous region consists of characteristic black-to-red granite. Each gabion was made up of rocks contained in a steel netting cube with each dimension approximately two metres in length. Depending on the threat, bunkers were commonly protected by eight to 10m of rock gabions that made the positions virtually immune to artillery rounds and bombs.

Accordingly, hygiene and cleanliness were of the highest priority. Paper plates and plastic cutlery were used for all meals and then burnt to reduce the risk of gastro-enteritis and other stomach disorders while fresh water was dispensed from underground pipes running from controlled clean supplies pumped from inland for drinking and showering. Each *Maoz* had a resident doctor to maintain standards of hygiene, provide medical care and sustain the welfare of the soldiers. Often a reserve officer serving his annual 30-days of reserve duty, he was usually older and more mature than his charges, so he also acted as a surrogate parent and counsellor since a doctor was not within the tactical chain of command inside the strongpoint. As part of the welfare considerations, all troops in the *Maozim* were encouraged to make contact with their families on a daily basis using the military communications network that is linked to the government-controlled civilian telephone service. Similarly, mail and newspapers were delivered every day – artillery bombardments allowing – and the troops were regularly distracted by entertainers and informative lectures on all manner of subjects to relieve the boredom and sense of isolation.

Days were spent cleaning and checking weapons; keeping a constant watch on enemy positions and logging any changes in their defence works or dispositions while maintaining one's own defence works not least of which was keeping the ever-encroaching sand at bay. When time allowed the occasional football match acted as a diversion from the endless games of *sheshbesh* or backgammon in the underground bunkers when under fire. As so much time was spent underground during the War of Attrition, the Israeli troops called themselves 'moles' and often a soldier would return from his tour of duty in the *Maozim* far paler than when he arrived. All troops serving in the Bar Lev Line, usually for three months at a time, were given regular periods of leave. From the Sinai, they were flown back to Israel by civilian aircraft and then transported home at government expense. With their experiences on the front line, they sometimes found themselves wincing when vehicles backfired and occasionally even hurled themselves to the ground out of habit. The respite of leave allowed time for relaxing and satisfying other appetites. As one reserve captain who spent three months on the line remarked: 'Down there you just don't think about sex. It's probably the tension.'

A cook prepares food at a *Maoz* including a jorum of tomatoes – that absolute staple of the Israeli diet without which no meal would be complete. Indeed, the IDF Quartermaster, Major-General Matityahu Peled, bitterly complained that many of his men were being sacrificed for the sake of transporting tomatoes to the Bar Lev Line when supply trucks ran into ambushes or were the victims of mines; one of the hidden costs of supporting the static strongpoints of the Bar Lev Line.

EYES HAVE THEY BUT THEY SEE NOT, PSALM 135: 16

Within two months of the ceasefire, President Nasser died of a heart attack on 28 September 1970 and was succeeded by his vice president, Anwar al-Sadat. Like his predecessor, President Sadat was determined to reclaim the lost lands of the Sinai by any means possible be they political or military. However, his extravagant pronouncements that he was willing 'to sacrifice a million Egyptian lives' to achieve these ends and his continuing prevarication when 1971 was to have been 'The Year of Decision' only tended to reinforce Israeli perceptions that he was a weak leader. Nevertheless, with no political progress through 1971 and into 1972, President Sadat decided that war was the only remaining option in November 1972. His expulsion of thousands of Soviet military advisers from Egypt in July had galvanized the Kremlin into providing more sophisticated weaponry such as the T-62 MBT in large numbers as well as the highly effective SA-6 anti-aircraft missile system. Detailed planning for a limited war now began.

Despite a general improvement in the quality of the armed forces, the Egyptian high command remained fully aware of the strengths of the IDF, particularly their superiority in the air and in manoeuvre warfare. The former was to be contained by the rapidly expanding Air Defence Command and the latter was to be broken by an unprecedented deployment of anti-tank guided weapons in the front lines, as discussed previously. In order to maximize the performance of the Malyutka or Sagger missiles, these were employed by highly trained soldiers from the artillery branch that were attached to the infantry divisions as a concerted screen against any armoured attack. Fundamental to the plan, codenamed *High Minarets*, was for the Egyptian army to attack across the Suez Canal on a broad front and secure an extensive lodgement in the Sinai Desert while remaining under the missile umbrella of SA-75 and S-125 SAM sites on the western bank of the canal: a distance of no more than 16km. The political logjam would thus be broken and a negotiated settlement could then follow. The assault was to be coordinated with a major offensive by the Syrian Army to regain the Golan Heights so as to force the IDF to fight on two fronts simultaneously. But first, the formidable obstacles of the Suez Canal and the sand ramparts protecting the Bar Lev Line had to be overcome.

Major-General Gamal Mohamed Ali fought in the 1948, 1956 and 1967 Arab-Israeli Wars and was Commander of the Engineer Corps before and during the October War of 1973, so it is only appropriate that his recollections of Egyptian preparations should be recounted in what became a remarkable feat of arms:

> The crossing of the Suez Canal – the largest water barrier ever traversed in the history of warfare – could not have been completed successfully without overcoming another barrier on the eastern bank. This was the enormous fortified artificial sand barrier that extended along the Bar Lev line. This barrier ranged from eight to 20m in height and was eight to 10m deep. The barrier was equipped with tank and direct fire positions and interspersed with fortified positions at approximately four kilometre intervals along its entire length from Port Tewfiq to East Qantara. It was made of a highly compact mixture of sand and mud. The sand barrier was one of the greatest challenges before the Egyptian command and military planners. We would have to create

breaches in order to allow for the passage of forces and military equipment, without which we would not be able to mount a successful penetration of the other side. So formidable was it that Moshe Dayan, former Israeli minister of defence, said, 'It would take the American and Soviet engineer corps, together, to break through the Bar Lev line.' Soviet experts at the time said that what was needed was an atom bomb.

'We conducted numerous experiments in order to determine the best way to overcome the barrier at a site on the Damietta branch of the Nile. First we tried explosives, which were ineffective. Then we tried artillery and mortar fire, but to no avail. Mechanical equipment was too slow and clumsy. It was at this point that we thought of water guns. Many of our officers had participated in the construction of the High Dam where they helped transport five million cubic metres of sand using enormous hydraulic pumps that could suck up 50 cubic meters of Nile water per hour, directing it in a powerful

The old military adage of always occupying the high ground is graphically illustrated in these photographs of IDF observation posts guarding the vital Mitla and Gidi passes that were the gateways to central Sinai and from thereon to Israel. From these heights it was possible to see as far as the Suez Canal. (Stuart Bracken)

stream onto mountains of sand which quickly turned into a very liquid mud that could then be piped into sedimentation beds. It was this same technology that we would bring to bear on the sand barrier at the Bar Lev line. We conducted our first experiment with water guns at the Wardan Canal near Qanater [in the Nile Delta]. It was a great success, but the equipment we had brought up from the High Dam was too bulky. We therefore purchased several 100hp turbine pumps weighing 205kg each from a German company. These we fitted out with hoses and placed them in 1.5-ton capacity boats.'

After buying two water pumps for experimental purposes, a further 100 were purchased from the West German firm of Magirus Deutz in May 1972, ostensibly for the Cairo fire department. As a bulk purchase, the quoted price was 30,000 Dm each or $12,500, so for the price of a single MBT the Egyptians devised and perfected a secret weapon that was to allow their whole strategic offensive to succeed. Yet water pumps would have no effect against an Israeli secret weapon installed on the Bar Lev Line. The brainchild of Colonel David Lascov, at 66 the oldest IDF officer on active duty, large oil tanks were buried deep underground as protection against shellfire with pipes leading to the Suez Canal. At the first sign of an Egyptian attack, oil would be pumped across the surface of the water and then ignited, immolating any boat or vehicle that attempted to cross the canal. Codenamed *Dusky Light*, the system was installed at Forts Matzmed and Hizayon and underwent a spectacular demonstration in February 1971. The sheet of flames and swirling clouds of black smoke certainly alarmed the Egyptians but the IDF high command was less impressed. The results were deemed to be disappointing with the fire not covering sufficient area and burning out too soon. Accordingly, only dummy systems were installed in 16 of the other *Maozim* as a deterrent that the Egyptians took very seriously.

As the War of Attrition came to an end there were several significant changes of command in the higher echelons of the IDF. Chief of Staff, General Haim Bar-Lev was superseded by General David 'Dado' Elazar on 1 January 1970 while in Southern Command, the new GOC was Major-General Ariel Sharon. During his tenure in command up until the summer of 1973, General Sharon closed down 15 of the original 31 strongpoints. Meanwhile, he extended the network of roads across the Sinai Peninsula to support his belief in the time-honoured IDF doctrine that the battle must be taken into enemy territory at the earliest opportunity. To this end, the sand ramparts were thinned down on the Israeli side at selected points and extensive assembly areas were constructed nearby surrounded by sand berms to provide protection to an invasion force poised to cross the canal 'into Africa'. To support this enterprise, General Tal instigated the procurement of engineer bridging equipment on the international market and at home. The latter included the construction of a massive 200m-long, 400-ton Gesher Haglilim or Roller Bridge, another creation from the fertile brain of Colonel Lascov, that was towed by a fleet of 16 tanks at a speed of just a few miles of hour and then only over fairly level terrain and in a mainly straight line; hence the need for special straight roads such as Akavish and Tirtur. Together, Generals Tal and Sharon produced the keys to victory in the forthcoming conflict although these innovative means still needed the Bar Lev Line to achieve their ends. More curiously, General Sharon invested heavily in a secondary line of strongholds behind the Bar Lev Line that became known as *Taozim*. Like the *Maozim*, these were constructed from concrete blocks reinforced by several metres of rock-filled gabions. They were intended to provide cover for armoured and infantry units assigned to Operation *Dovecote* in the staging areas close to the Artillery Road and to be manned by reservists during periods of heightened tension. During the October War of 1973, they served

The maintenance of morale among the troops stationed on the Bar Lev Line was of considerable importance to the IDF and great efforts were made to keep them entertained as well as fit for combat. Here, the celebrated theatre and film actress, Aviva Orgad, conducts a performance during the War of Attrition on 5 November 1969. On 9 January 1970, the renowned illusionist, Uri Geller, performed for troops on the Bar Lev Line. Such was the success of his show that he was asked to repeat his feats of bending keys et al. before the GOC Southern Command, Major-General Ariel Sharon, that night. Thereafter the two became firm friends.

no real purpose yet absorbed a significant proportion of the total costs of the defensive infrastructure of the Sinai Peninsula, estimated to be $500 million of which $200 million was spent on the Bar Lev Line itself.

Despite these elaborate defensive arrangements in the Sinai Peninsula and the Golan Heights, the IDF was falling prey to the sophisticated Arab deception plan that was unfolding with consummate skill, compounded by their own complacent assessment of the politico-military situation in the Middle East. Essentially, the Israelis did not believe that the Egyptians would attack until such time as they had achieved at least parity in air power and even then would not undertake any offensive without the support of Syria and other Arab nations. Israeli military intelligence estimated that such a likelihood to be 'highly improbable' until at least 1976. By now the hard-fought lessons of the War of Attrition had been largely forgotten, although highly complex and elaborate plans had been devised to defeat the Arab air defence systems, codenamed *Tagar* on the Egyptian front and *Dougman 5* on the Syrian front. The IAF now maintained that it could destroy the Syrian air force 'in two hours' and if the Egyptians launched an offensive across the Suez Canal it would be contained by Israeli armour while the IAF destroyed their air defence system within 'a day or two', allowing the IDF ground forces to cross the canal on day two or three at the latest. This sense of superiority was reinforced by an air battle over the Golan Heights on 13 September 1973 when 13 Syrian aircraft were shot down at the cost of just one Israeli plane. This incident did allow the Syrian Army to reinforce the Golan Heights with more ground troops and tank battalions but Israeli military intelligence misread this as just a reaction to the air battle. Similarly,

The fate of the *Maozim*

Egyptian name	Israeli name	Personnel	Extra troops	Escape attempt	Attacked	KIA	WIA	Troops evacuated	Date & time, evacuation	Date & time, surrender
	Budapest	63	8	N	Y	3	0		N/A	
Km 10	Orkal 1	20	8	Y	Y	39	19	5	07 1700	
Km 10	Orkal 2	17		Y	Y	As above	As above	As above	As above	
Km 10	Orkal 3	19		Y	Y	As above	As above	As above	As above	
Km 19	Lazanit	17		N	Y	9	8			07 1700
El Tina	Drora	19		Y	Artillery	3	1	15	07 1430	
El Cap	Ketuba	21		Y	Artillery	2		19	07 1400	
Kantara	Milano	28	15	Y	Y	13	6	24	08 0600	
El Ballah	Mifreket	16		Y	Y	5	7	5	07 1700	
El Firdan	Hizayon	20		N	Y	12	8			09 0900
Ismailia	Purkan	33		Y	Y			33	09 0230	
Deversoir	Matzmed	34		N	Y	2	32			09 0800
Tel Salam	Lakekan	10		Y	Artillery			10	08 0300	
Kabrit	Botzer	26	12	Y	Artillery			38	09 0200	
Shalofa	Lituf	29		Y	Y	18	11			07 1330
El Shatt	Mafzeah	28		N	Y	5	23			08 1400
El Gabbasat	Nisan	20		N	Y	10	10			09 1500
Quai	Masreq	30	12	Y	Y	5	37			13 1100

With an FN MAG 60.20 7.62mm general purpose machine gun ready to hand, an M3 half-track conducts a patrol along a track bordering the Suez Canal. Since the *Maozim* were commonly some 15km apart, it was necessary to mount daily patrols between them to monitor the ground that remained unobserved from the strongpoints and to check for any Egyptian incursions into the Sinai Peninsula.

the major troop concentrations along the Suez Canal were dismissed as the usual autumn manoeuvres known as Tahrir. Reports from local intelligence officers on both the Bar Lev and Purple lines were ignored. This blindness to read the many military intelligence signals indicating that war was imminent was later termed the 'Konseptziya' or 'the preconception': the assumption that the enemy would only do what the Israelis thought they would do. It was a catastrophic failure of intelligence and was to cost the personnel manning the Bar Lev Line dearly.

BREAKING THE LINE

Yom Kippur, or the Day of Atonement, is the most important festival in the Judaic religious calendar. In 1973, it fell on Saturday 6 October, coinciding with the Sabbath. This was the date chosen by the Egyptian high command to launch Operation *Sharara* or *Spark* in conjunction with the Syrian Army. The codename for the assault across the Suez Canal was Operation *Badr* after the first victory of the Prophet Mohammed in AD 624. The day gave the optimum combination of tidal flow and currents in the canal and sufficient moonlight to allow bridging operations to continue through the night: any later and the chances of snow on the Golan Heights would be too high. It was also assumed that the Israelis would be at a low level of preparedness on such a day when even the radio and television stations were closed down. For many months previously, the Egyptians had been building enormous sand ramparts that were far higher than their counterparts on the Bar Lev Line. From their dominating heights, observation was possible deep into the Sinai as far as the Artillery Road and they also overlooked the *Maozim* positions. By their very size they obscured any direct observation by the Israelis beyond the far bank of the canal. Military intelligence had dismissed them as purely a labour project for Egyptian conscripts and they were known derisively as the 'Pyramids'. However, they now contained hull-down firing positions for direct-fire weapons as well as firing pits for Sagger teams to engage Israeli armour rushing to the aid of the Bar Lev Line. Rather than enlarge their own sand ramparts as a countermeasure, the Israelis built a number of tank revetments some 1,000 to 1,500m opposite them so as to destroy any AFVs or troops on the ramparts by superior long-range gunnery techniques. Because of their shape these revetments were known as 'fins'. Behind the imposing bulk of the Pyramids, the Egyptians concentrated their assault forces and their equipment away from the prying eyes of the Israelis.

F 155MM GUN EMPLACEMENT

The Bar Lev Line was not just a string of strongpoints along the Suez Canal but a sophisticated series of field fortifications stretching deep into the Sinai Peninsula supported by an extensive road network to replenish and support the far-flung positions. During the War of Attrition a second line of strongholds known as *Taozim* was constructed on the ridgeline behind the Artillery Road some eight to ten kilometres inland from the canal. The *Taozim* were to be manned by reservists during any period of emergency. Most of these were capable of housing an infantry company. As the anchor at the southern end of the Bar Lev Line, there was a completely different *Taoz* that incorporated six 155mm howitzers in heavily armoured encasements. These powerful guns dominated the southern entrance of the Suez Canal as well as Suez City itself. The steel and concrete structure of the gun emplacements was encased in multiple layers of rock gabions with further ones to the front to reduce obscuration on firing and absorb shell splinters from counterbattery fire. The guns could be withdrawn inside the emplacements with steel shutters that could be lowered to protect the weapons against counterbattery fire. The whole structure was covered by camouflage netting to blend it in with the surrounding desert while powerful fans dispelled gun fumes through ventilator pipes poking through the roof.

155mm gun emplacement

47

These comprised two field armies, the Second and Third, with five infantry divisions and several independent brigades, both armour and infantry, backed by three mechanized and two armoured divisions. In addition, there were independent tank brigades, two paratroop brigades, a marine brigade and some 28 battalions of commandos, as well as numerous battalions of the vital combat engineers to breach the Bar Lev Line. The Egyptian Second Army was deployed along the Suez Canal from Lake Manzale to the Great Bitter Lake with the Third Army onwards to the Gulf of Suez. In total, there were some 180,000 troops, 2,200 tanks and 2,000 artillery pieces lining the Suez Canal. These were protected from air attack by the densest air defence system in the world with 130 SAM sites comprising SA-2, SA-3 and SA-6 SAM systems integrated with numerous AAA batteries. Within three hours of the initial crossing, each division was to have deployed to its front as a counter to Israeli armour some 314 RPGs (effective out to 500m); 108 57mm recoilless rifles (effective out to 1,600m) and 48 Sagger launchers with an effective range out to 3,000m. In addition there were scores of tanks, self-propelled guns and supplementary Sagger teams in overwatch from the sand ramparts on the western side of the canal. Combined with the thorough training and higher motivation of their troops, the Egyptian armed forces now had a formidable answer to the IAF and IAC.

On 15 June 1973, Major-General Shmuel 'Gorodish' Gonen became GOC Southern Command in place of General Sharon. This coincided with a number of other changes in the top postings within the IDF that resulted in a number of relatively inexperienced field commanders in place at the outset of the October War. Technically competent and personally brave, General Gonen was an armour officer who was a stickler for detail and had an abrasive not to say abusive manner with subordinates. He could hardly have been more different than the mercurial General Sharon who inspired total loyalty in his men: the latter now took command of a reserve division in time of war within Southern Command. After almost three years of 'No War No Peace', the purpose of the Bar Lev Line had become even more clouded. Many in the high command believed that in a general offensive the line would be quickly overwhelmed but military intelligence indicated that such a prospect remained 'highly improbable'. Since there had been no artillery bombardments for three years, maintenance of the infrastructure of the forts had declined as the IDF sought to reduce its overall expenditure. However the political imperative did not allow them to be abandoned. Accordingly there was no coherent policy as to the role of the Bar Lev Line in time of war except as outlined by its namesake on leaving his post as Chief of Staff: 'Its day-to-day mission is to prevent a serious breaching of the canal but the system can easily be turned into a jumping-off point.' The former was hardly possible if over half of the forts had been closed down. General Gonen soon decided to reopen 14 of them as well as build long-range observation towers in order to see over the sand rampart 'Pyramids'. But it was to prove too late. Similarly he ordered his chief of engineers to reactivate the *Dusky Light* 'fire on the water' weapon system that had not been maintained since 1971 and was now inoperable. An engineering team commanded by Second Lieutenant Shimon Tal arrived at the Hizayon strongpoint on the morning of Saturday 6 October – Yom Kippur.

Just days before, most of the regular troops manning the Bar Lev Line were relieved so that they could go home for Rosh Hashana and Yom Kippur. Their replacements were reservists drawn from the 116th 'Etzioni' Brigade based in Jerusalem, which had never before been assigned to the Suez Canal.

None were happy at the prospect of military service away from their families over the religious holiday. Many were in their late 30s and some had virtually no training at all since they were recent immigrants to Israel: some even could hardly speak Hebrew. Nevertheless, it was just for a month and then their annual tour of duty would be over. They arrived at the forts festooned with books, fishing rods and *sheshbesh* boards to alleviate the boredom. Captain Motti Ashkenazi, the commander of Moaz Budapest on the Mediterranean coast, even brought his German Shepherd puppy called Peng. However, Captain Ashkenazi had severe reservations as to the state of the defence works at Budapest and immediately demanded more barbed wire, sandbags and mines. He was also dismayed at the arrogance of the resident brigade intelligence officer who had conducted their briefing given prior to deployment. When asked the question by a sergeant: 'What will happen if the Egyptians simply decide to roll forward? We wouldn't even know. The first warning would be when they crush us.' The disdainful answer came back: 'When someone farts in Cairo, we hear it in Tel Aviv. We'll have plenty of time to replace you with regular units if and when we think something is about to happen. Even if they surprise us and cross over,' continued the intelligence officer, 'the air force and armored divisions will give them the heave-ho half an hour afterwards!' The reality was to be very different.

Against the combined might of the Second and Third Egyptian armies, there were just 450 troops manning the Bar Lev Line including a few supplementary soldiers such as Lieutenant Tal's engineering team while the three southernmost *Maozim* were manned by regular troops. There was only one platoon of three Magach (M48) tanks deployed along the canal at Maoz Orkal at the extreme north of the line. To the rear, along the Artillery Road were the 91 tanks of the 14th Armoured Brigade under the command of Colonel Amnon Reshef. In support were 12 artillery batteries, each of four guns, including one battery each of M107 175mm self-propelled guns and M109 155mm self-propelled howitzers, together with a further six batteries of Israeli-manufactured M50 155mm self-propelled howitzers as well as further batteries of Soltam 160mm and 120mm self-propelled mortars. In addition there were the 11 *Taozim*

The Egyptians acquired their first SAM system from the Soviet Union in 1965 and, by the outbreak of the Six Day War, 27 batteries of the SA-75K Dvina (SA-2 Guideline) were in service. Following the war, the network was greatly expanded and on 1 July 1968 all SAM systems came under the control of the Air Defence Command that was separate from the Egyptian Air Force. Based on the Soviet PVO-Strany model, the new command also controlled two brigades of MiG-21 interceptors as the Egyptians attempted to gain air superiority over the Suez Canal. Such a division of resources led to some friction and mutual recrimination, which was exacerbated by the often difficult working relationship between the Egyptian armed forces and their Soviet advisors. This is the combination of the SA-75MK Dvina on its SM-63-1 launcher and the RSNA-75M (Fan Song B) fire-control radar. (Lon Nordeen)

secondary fortifications manned by service personnel. While never truly part of the Bar Lev Line, the *Taoz* named Tzeider at the extreme south of the line incorporated six French Obusier de 155mm Modele 50 howitzers in fortified emplacements that were capable of bombarding Suez City and providing fire support to positions such as Masreq and Nisan. To the east were almost 200 tanks of the Sinai Division under the command of Major-General Albert Mendler to give a grand total of 290 together with approximately 18,000 troops. Unfortunately, only the understrength 14th Armored Brigade was deployed forwards with the two other brigades in reserve rather than two forwards and one in reserve as required by *Shovach Yonim*. Such was the complacency induced by the 'Konseptziya'. With no reserves to hand and few regular troops manning the Bar Lev Line, Plan *Dovecote* was coming apart at the seams. On 5 October, scores of Egyptian reconnaissance teams, some dressed as Bedouin tribesmen, crossed the canal to conduct a final intelligence assessment as to recent Israeli redeployments. The scouts radioed back: 'The Israelis are asleep'. That night frogmen swam across the canal and blocked all the fuel outlet pipes, be they real or dummy, of the *Dusky Light* weapon system. The Egyptians were leaving nothing to chance.

At 1405hrs on 6 October 1973, an artillery bombardment of unprecedented ferocity fell on the strongpoints of the Bar Lev Line. Some 2,000 guns opened up along the entire front with 10,500 shells striking Israeli positions in the first minute at a rate of 175 rounds a second. Meanwhile, EAF fighter bombers, Scud and FROG surface-to-surface missiles struck targets further east while heliborne commandos flew deep into the Sinai to intercept Israeli reinforcements. In a massive barrage lasting 53 minutes, some 3,000 tons of high explosive saturated the *Moazim*: the weapon of choice to attack the well-protected bunkers being the Soviet M-55 240mm heavy mortar with its 288lb projectile. At 1415hrs, 720 rubber dinghies took to the water transporting the first assault troops across the canal to cries of 'Allahu akhbar' – 'God is the greatest' – as they paddled their heavily laden craft. Most of these troops crossed at points not covered by fire from the *Maozim* but even so the Egyptian artillery isolated the strongpoints further with a sustained barrage of smoke shells. So acrid was the dense yellow smoke that many defenders thought that the Egyptians were using poison gas. After instructing the troops at Maoz Hizayon as how to ignite the *Dusky Light* system with incendiary grenades, the unfortunate Lieutenant Tal, who had only arrived at the front that morning, was on his way to Matzmed when the assault began. He became the first POW to be captured.

Initially, the Egyptian assault troops bypassed the *Maozim* as they rushed to take up their allotted fire positions at the tank 'fins' beyond the Bar Lev Line but once the artillery barrage subsided many of the strongpoints were subjected to ground attack. The fate of the *Maozim* depended to a large degree on the level of leadership. Those where the officers or senior NCOs became early casualties tended to lack a cohesive defence. In those strongpoints where the troops manned the firing pits as soon as possible, Egyptian casualties were significant. There were extraordinary acts of bravery and some of cowardice: of men broken in will by the force of the bombardment; of slovenly, insubordinate private soldiers in peacetime that became natural leaders in the crucible of battle. Soon after the assault began, desperate radio messages were being transmitted from the *Maozim*:

> The Egyptians bombed Tassa and Mafzeah. ... Egyptian tanks mounted the ramps [on the west bank of the Suez Canal] and have opened fire on us. ... They are shooting at Milano and Masreq. ... An aerial attack on Sharm. Antiaircraft activated. ... Shelling on Um Chashiva [the Southern Command war room]. ... Egyptians crossing south to Hizayon. ... Pressure on the strongholds. Gunfire battles under way. Reports of Egyptian infiltration at Agam Chemer Hakatan. ... Attempts to cross opposite all of the strongholds. No more forces in the sector. At Mifreket there was an Egyptian crossing. No wireless communication with Orkal. Eight tanks totally taken out of commission at Budapest. Two of our tanks located at Budapest. One in operation. One barrel [self-propelled artillery weapon] out of commission at Budapest. ... Nisan under infantry attack. ... Movement on the Jidi Road. One hundred Egyptians are mounting Lituf. At Hizayon the attack was repelled. Many dead and wounded.

'Request air force assistance the length of the northern sector,' came an officer's voice over the radio. 'Egyptians present at Mifreket, Lazanit and Milano Aleph ... Lazanit and Mifreket overtaken. Request aerial assistance urgently in the northern sector ... No contact with Budapest and Orkal. ...

In the southern sector the situation is good, except for an incursion onto the Gidi Road. No incursions at central [sector]. At northern [sector] the situation is bad. The strongholds have been captured.'

Reflecting the informal nature between ranks in the IDF, there were persistent and repeated calls of 'I need Benny': Major-General Benny Peled being the commander of the IAF. But after a number of largely ineffectual ground-attack missions along the Suez Canal, the Phantoms and Skyhawks were diverted to the Northern Front where the situation was even more desperate after the Syrians had penetrated the Purple Line in force. The *Maozim* were left to their own devices.

None of the positions surrendered or were evacuated without the express orders of higher command. The first to fall was Lituf at 1330hrs on Sunday 7 October: the last was Masreq on the Quay at Port Tewfiq at 1100hrs on 13 October. From the outset, Southern Command despatched tank formation after tank formation towards the Suez Canal in a vain attempt to bolster the defences of the Bar Lev Line but invariably they fell victim to the swarming Egyptian anti-tank teams hiding in every hollow and sand dune. By dawn on 7 October, the Sinai Division had lost 180 tanks, by the evening over 100 more. That is one tank for virtually every casualty sustained in the *Maozim*. Of the 14 tanks despatched to Milano, only five returned. Of the 18 despatched to Mifreket, only another five returned. If their purpose had been to evacuate the troops in the strongpoints, there might have been some sense in their sacrifice. Of the three Magach tanks at Orkal, two remained mobile when the garrison received permission to break out on Sunday afternoon, 7 October. Together with an M3 half-track, the survivors from the three Orkal positions charged through the surrounding Egyptian infantry. After a couple of miles, they picked up some other stragglers but after a few hundred yards the two rearmost vehicles were hit by RPG fire. In the lead tank, the

As the desperate defence of the Sinai Peninsula continues, an IDF armoured unit moves off as dawn breaks on the third day of the Yom Kippur War, 9 October 1973. That evening just such a unit discovered the gap between the Egyptian Second and Third armies that created the opportunity for the IDF to mount a concerted counteroffensive across the Suez Canal.

commander, Sergeant Shlomo Arman, reported the ambush and was about to go to their aid when his company commander directed: 'Negative. Keep moving! They'll kill you all. Move out of there fast. Out.' The tank moved off along the darkened road through the swampy salt marshes only to be hit in turn by an RPG. The surviving crew and passengers bailed out and struggled onwards towards Israeli lines. Around midnight the five remaining men saw the outline of Israeli tanks to their front. Sergeant Arman called out: 'Hey tankers we're from the forts.' In an exchange familiar to soldiers across the world, the reply came: 'Don't move! Who are you?' 'We're from Orkal.' 'Who knows you?' Arman gave the names of his battalion and brigade commanders. 'Where in Israel are you from?' A number of other questions about everyday life followed ending with: 'What company are you from?' 'L Company' Arman responded. To which came: 'What company did you say?' 'L Company.' Suddenly a 105mm high-explosive round exploded beside the five men, killing the gallant Sergeant Arman and a fellow crewman and wounding two others. It was a shocking misfortune after such a harrowing ordeal.

Herein lies the tragedy of the Bar Lev Line. The failure of the IDF high command to define its role in time of general warfare condemned the strongpoints to annihilation and with it the men that manned them and those recklessly despatched to reinforce them. Almost without exception, every assumption made by the IDF prior to the war about Arab intentions and capabilities proved to be erroneous. From the cataclysmic failure of military intelligence, through the containment of the IAF with multiple missile strikes to the inability of the IAC to crush the Arab 'chiri biri' or 'rotten infantry' under their tracks, Plan *Dovecote* lay shattered in the burning hulks of tanks in the desert and the battered remnants of the Bar Lev Line. In all, 126 men died defending the forts and 161 others were taken prisoner. But then, perhaps their sacrifice was not in vain. The Egyptians expected to incur 30,000 casualties in the storming of the Bar Lev Line when in fact they suffered just 208 dead. Nevertheless, the delay imposed by the stubborn defence and the time taken to create breaches in the sand ramparts in the Third Army sector meant that the Egyptian bridgeheads were neither as extensive nor contiguous as required by Operation *High Minarets*. The ensuing operational pause to absorb the early Israeli counterattacks allowed Israeli reserves to be rushed to the front faster than expected but did not allow the bridgeheads to be consolidated. Within days three Israeli armoured divisions were mustered in the Sinai. Furthermore, the failure to form a seamless bridgehead between the Second and Third armies was ruthlessly exploited by General Sharon in his unrelenting quest to take the war into enemy territory.

Ironically, it was the Egyptians that clutched defeat from the jaws of victory. Operations *Badr* and *High Minarets* had been an outstanding success and achieved the stated aims of the political leadership by creating a comprehensive Egyptian military presence in the Sinai. At a time when the Israelis were seriously considering a ceasefire in place, President Sadat ordered a general offensive codenamed *Granite 2*, much to the dismay of his high command, in an attempt to gain the vital passes in central Sinai and

One of the leading players in the story of the Bar Lev Line was Major-General Ariel Sharon. After commanding one of the *ugdas* or divisions that captured the Sinai Peninsula during the Six Day War in 1967, he returned to the Sinai as GOC Southern Command between 1970 and 1973 when he was in charge of the Bar Lev Line. Despite reservations in some quarters, Sharon closed 16 *Maozim* while constructing a second line of strongholds and extending the road network to allow easier movement of tanks and equipment to the Suez Canal in preparation for any attack into Egypt. The reduction in the number of *Maozim* allowed the Egyptians to study the configuration of the strongpoints that provided essential intelligence for when they attacked in earnest in October 1973 by when Maj. Gen. Sharon had retired from the army and entered politics. Nevertheless, he returned to duty during the Yom Kippur War in command of 143rd Reserve Armored Division and he is shown here in his M3 command vehicle.

A Maoz under attack during the October War of 1973

A *MAOZ* UNDER ATACK DURING THE OCTOBER WAR OF 1973

On 6 October 1973, the Egyptian armed forces achieved total strategic and tactical surprise when they launched a massive ground assault against the Bar Lev Line. With just 450 defenders in the *Maozim*, the Israeli positions were systematically overwhelmed in the coming days. The tenacity of the defenders, and indeed the attackers, varied from *Maoz* to *Maoz* but within days all fell to the enemy or were evacuated. Yet the *Maozim* were never designed to repel a full-scale attack – that was the role of the standing armoured formations in the Sinai Desert and the IAF together with the rapidly mobilized reserves. In the event this is what happened but the sacrifice and loss of the men in the *Maozim* came as a severe shock to the people of Israel. Many of the defenders fought to the last from their prepared positions such as those shown here with .50-cal. heavy machine guns firing from the prefabricated steel tubs that formed the standard weapons pit. The three-man 81mm mortar crew are serving their weapon in a larger steel tub with its need for greater ammunition storage. Extensive barbed-wire entanglements that incorporated numerous anti-personnel landmines protected every position. However mines were generally ineffective as the shifting sands generally exposed them to the observant eye. Nevertheless the Egyptians were well prepared and the wire entanglements were breached by Bangalore torpedoes, seen at extreme left. Across the canal can be seen the 'Pyramids' that dominated the *Maozim* with direct fire weapons and for observation.

supposedly to relieve pressure on his Syrian ally. In an ill-conceived, ill-coordinated armoured thrust on a wide front beyond the umbrella of their SAM defences, the Egyptians allowed themselves to be drawn into the type of manoeuvre warfare in which the IDF excelled. In the space of a few hours over 200 Egyptian tanks were destroyed in the largest armoured encounter since the battle of Kursk at a cost to the Israelis of just over 20 tanks. Arguably, this was the very defensive doctrine that the IDF should have adopted in the first place rather than being stymied by the static Bar Lev Line. Thereafter the initiative passed to the Israelis. The Bar Lev Line had one more service to play when Maoz Matzmed became the hinge for the major counter-offensive across the Suez Canal that allowed the IDF to win a brilliant tactical victory on the battlefield by surrounding the Egyptian Third Army.

Back to the Purple Line

At the outset of the war, the Israelis on the Golan Heights faced the same vastly disproportionate level of enemy forces as in the Sinai. Like the Bar Lev Line, the fortifications along the Purple Line were intended as well-protected observation posts and fighting positions against minor incursions by enemy patrols. They also acted as artillery fire-control centres when Syrian forces conducted a 'battle day' incursion in strength. Each of the ten strongpoints or *Mutzavim* along the Purple Line had a complement of 12 to 30 men but, unlike the Bar Lev Line, the northern five were manned by infantry of the elite Golani Brigade and the others by regular soldiers of the 50th Paratroop Battalion, as well as intelligence and artillery personnel. Again, each position was to be defended by a platoon of tanks in time of hostilities with elevated firing ramps close by to allow the long-range destruction of enemy armour in well-prepared killing zones. The Syrian offensive on the Golan Heights was conducted by three mechanized and two armoured divisions; a total of almost 1,400 tanks against just 177 Shot (Centurion) MBTs. Displaying a dogged determination and commitment unseen before, the massed ranks of Syrian T-55s smashed into the Israeli lines under the cover of an intense artillery barrage and an extensive SAM umbrella.

The Shot tanks of the 188th 'Barak' Brigade rushed forward to the aid of the strongpoints and from their elevated ramps exacted an awful slaughter of Syrian AFVs but still they surged forward. Despite heavy casualties, the Syrians eventually breached the Israeli anti-tank ditch and minefields; the strongpoints were invariably bypassed and suppressed by artillery barrages.

Major-General 'Bren' Adan briefs Minister of Defense Moshe Dayan about the final battle for Suez City two days after the end of the Yom Kippur War. From the outset of the war, Maj. Gen. Adan was in command of the 252nd Armored Division that fought the defensive battle plan as ordained by Operation *Dovecote*. His division lost numerous tanks and many men in repeated attempts to support the defenders of the Bar Lev Line. Following the decisive holding battle of 14 October, his division spearheaded the Israeli counteroffensive 'into Africa' culminating in the isolation of the Egyptian Third Army. As the original architect of the Bar Lev Line, his sheer professionalism in the difficult days of the Yom Kippur War up to victory some three weeks later marked him as the outstanding commander within Southern Command during the war.

Nevertheless, they inflicted numerous casualties on the advancing Syrian units while the artillery spotters brought down accurate fire on concentrations of tanks and vehicles. So effective was their defence that when Major-General Yitzhak 'Haka' Hofi, GOC Northern Command, ordered the strongpoints to be evacuated during the evening of 6 October both Colonel Amir Drori, commander of the Golani Brigade, and Major Yoram Yair commanding the paratroop contingent demurred. Such was the value of having regular troops manning the strongpoints. Although most positions were evacuated, some continued to resist such as Mutzavim 116 and Mutzavim 107 to the last until relieved in the general Israeli counteroffensive that regained the Purple Line and thrust into Syria to bring the war to the gates of Damascus.

AFTERMATH

The field fortifications of the Bar Lev Line on the Suez Canal and the Purple Line on the Golan Heights were conceived and constructed as an expedient measure to counter the specific menace of concentrated artillery fire from Egyptian and Syrian forces in contravention of ceasefire agreements. Their primary purpose was to reduce IDF casualties on the frontlines of Israel's greatly extended borders. During the War of Attrition from 1967 to 1970 that purpose was achieved but thereafter the role of the fortifications became muddled and confused; indeed a reflection in microcosm of the overall Israeli defence strategy that was hopelessly compromised by the arrogance and the blinkered perceptions of the 'Konseptziya'. There was no lack of intelligence of the impending Arab attack in October 1973 but there was a woeful lack of correct interpretation. The result was disaster in the opening days of the October War as Israeli tank platoons, companies and battalions mounted repeated futile counterattacks against the concerted missile screen along the length of the Suez Canal as did the Israeli Air Force. Frederick the Great stated: 'He who defends everything defends nothing.' It was not until after the *Maozim* of the Bar Lev Line either surrendered or were evacuated that the IDF recovered its composure. In the meantime, it was down to the courage and commitment of the individual Israeli soldier to rectify the disastrous situation in the Sinai and on the Golan Heights. That included the defenders trapped in the strongpoints under ferocious artillery bombardment and ground attack from a determined enemy.

The cost in casualties was high but the damage to Israeli self-esteem and confidence was even greater. No longer were the IDF the vaunted guardians of the Israeli people and the latter required answers to the failures of the October War. These demands were encapsulated by a single man standing outside the Prime Minister's office in Tel Aviv day after day in a lonely vigil with a placard condemning Golda Meir and Moshe Dyan. That man was Motti Ashkenazi, the reserve captain who had commanded Maoz Budapest. His lone protest grew until thousands thronged the streets leading to the resignation of two of Israel's the most revered politicians and the fall of the Labour Party after 29 years in power. The Bar Lev Line had claimed two more casualties but there were many others as survivors of the Bar Lev Line and the prisoners of war in particular succumbed to post traumatic stress disorder after their ghastly ordeal. It was as if the Bar Lev Line had become a symbol of the military and political failures of the October War. Conversely, for the Egyptians the assault across the Suez Canal and the capture of the Bar Lev Line in Operation *Badr* became a matter of immense pride and a shining example of the newfound prowess of the Arab soldier. To this day, 6 October is celebrated as Armed Forces Day. The psychology of victory or defeat is often more important than any analytical assessment of military success or failure on the battlefield.

This applied equally to the Israelis as it did to the Arabs. Following the Six Day War, Israeli arrogance and intransigence grew apace until they convinced themselves that they could defeat any combination of the massed Arab armies

As part of the Israel–Egypt Peace Treaty of 26 March 1979 following the Camp David Accords, the IDF began a phased withdrawal of the Sinai Peninsula that embraced over 170 separate military installations including the remnants of the Bar Lev Line. In a ceremony to mark the departure of the IDF from Refidim on 23 January 1980, Magach 6 MBTs pass a sign stating: 'We did not retreat. We leave in the name of peace.'

arrayed against them. This led to a critical reduction in the standing forces ready to resist any invasion. Similarly, the Egyptians became so obsessed with the difficulties of the assault crossing of the Suez Canal and the perceived strength of the Bar Lev Line that it became a barrier of fear, mentally as well as physically. Once the obstacle was overcome with relative ease, there was no flexibility or capacity to develop upon the unprecedented victory. Nevertheless, Egypt finally regained sovereignty over the Sinai Peninsula on 25 April 1982. This is now another national holiday celebrated as Sinai Liberation Day. The purpose of the War of Attrition and the Ramadan or October War of 1973 was achieved at last but at what a cost. These wars remain a damning indictment of the world's superpowers and the United Nations in their inability and lack of political will to resolve regional differences. The Bar Lev Line succeeded in its primary purpose and withstood over two years of ordeal by fire. It finally succumbed to water, delivered by high-pressure pumps and hoses, from the very waterway it was built to defend. As the renowned military thinker J. F. C. Fuller stated: 'History shows again and again that a combination of resistance and mobility – of shield and sword – is the true answer to mass.' The Bar Lev Line was the shield while the sword was wielded by the IAC and the IAF. The question as to whether there was a more suitable combination of shield and sword in October 1973 remains unanswered.

Thanks to his assignment with UNTSO, Major Stuart Bracken USMC had unrivalled access to the remnants of the Bar Lev Line and his researches have been fundamental in the production of this book. Here, he demonstrates the average depth of an Israeli trench line that would have been protected by multiple layers of sandbags on each side. As with much of the Bar Lev Line, simplicity of construction and materials was fundamental to allow rapid installation and repair as well as to reduce overall procurement costs. Some trench lines incorporated overhead metal hoops that were draped with hessian material to provide some measure of shade against the fearsome sun and to deny observation of troop movements to the Egyptians. (Stuart Bracken)

WALKING THE LINE

There are few people in the western world who have as much experience and knowledge of the Bar Lev Line as Major Stuart Bracken USMC who served in the Sinai Desert with UNTSO. Thanks to his unrivalled access and historical curiosity, an important record of the Bar Lev Line has been preserved for posterity. Without his selfless assistance this book would never have seen the light of day. Stuart Bracken recounts below his 'time on the line'. Created in the aftermath of the Israeli War of Independence in 1948, UNTSO was the first peacekeeping operation established by the United Nations. The main role of the military observers in the Middle East is to monitor ceasefires, supervise armistice agreements, prevent isolated incidents from escalating and to assist other UN peacekeeping operations in the region. There is a complementary organization on the Golan Heights along the Purple Line known as UNDOF or the United Nations Disengagement Observer Force that continues to supervise the implementation of the disengagement agreement between the Israelis and the Syrians.

In early 2003 I was seconded from the United States Marine Corps to the United Nations as the Operations Officer for the Observer Group Egypt (OGE). After three years of dreary staff work at US Joint Forces Command at Norfolk, Virginia, serving in the Sinai with UNTSO was just the tonic I needed. I had served previously with the United Nations in Cambodia, so I was aware of the importance of preparing for the mission by researching the topic in the minutest detail. Armed with my trusty credit card and my Amazon.com account, I set out to learn about the Sinai and UNTSO.

OGE's primary duty was to provide a UN presence throughout the Sinai, less the areas covered by the Multinational Force and Observers (MFO). Our patrols were carried out in two-vehicle teams and covered areas that had seen extensive battles between the IDF and the Egyptian army. The majority of the patrols were carried out within sight of the Suez Canal. As a result, the former positions of the Bar Lev Line were frequently visited during our duties.

Overlooking the shores of the Great Bitter Lake, Maoz Lakekan remains the best preserved of the strongpoints of the Bar Lev Line. It now incorporates a museum and after years of being an Egyptian Army facility is now open to the general public. This view illustrates one of the fundamental aspects of the strongpoints of the Bar Lev Line in that they were built upwards rather than downwards as is traditional in field fortifications because of the low water table due to the nearby Suez Canal and Bitter Lakes. (Stuart Bracken)

There is still some detritus of war along the Suez Canal such as this M48 Magach 3 that remains to this day beside the waterway that it fought to the death to defend with the 404m-wide Mubarak Peace Bridge spanning the canal some 70m above the water in the background. (Stuart Bracken)

Since the end of the 1973 Arab Israeli War several positions of the former Bar Lev Line have been preserved by the Egyptian Army as museums to document the Egyptian "victory" over the Israelis in 1973. The first of these positions I encountered was the former *Maoz* at Lakekan. In 2004 it was opened to the public at a charge of five Egyptian Pounds ($1.25). The position is maintained as it was supposed to have looked on 6 October 1973, right down to the dug-in tanks and the mannequin-served mortar positions. Soon after this, I became aware of the *Taoz* at Nozel and then the Fire Support Base at Tzeidar. Both of these positions are advertised from the road, but only Tzeidar was open to the public as of 2004 (five Egyptian Pound admission). I was soon hooked to find more of the 'lost' positions of the Bar Lev Line. Armed with a roadmap from Freytag & Berndt and the Osprey book The Yom Kippur War (Vol 2) by Simon Dunstan that travelled with me constantly, I made it a point to look for positions whenever my work took me in the vicinity of the Bar Lev Line. Needless to say, the Sinai was not to be as cooperative as I had hoped. The Bar Lev Line has suffered decades of abandonment, scavenging by locals and the shifting desert sands. Using my map of the Yom Kippur War and my GPS, I slowly began filling in the blanks, as I sought to find as many of the former positions as possible. Some positions, namely the *Taoz* at Notsa, jumped out at me from the Mitla Pass Road (Notsa was being made into a museum in 2004, and was fully operational in 2006). Other positions, such as the *Taoz* at Televizia did not become apparent until the week before I transferred from OGE to my new duties in Jerusalem.

Some of the biggest clues to finding the former positions of the Bar Lev Line were left by the Israelis themselves. These were the road systems built by the Israelis during their occupation of the Sinai. Especially helpful were the Lateral and Artillery roads. Although almost 40 years old, and never maintained after the Israeli withdrawal in 1982, the roads were in exceptional shape. After a period of time I could differentiate between the Israeli-made and the Egyptian-made roads. With the roads and the map from the book, I was able to identify roughly where the positions were, in relation to our patrol maps. The positions themselves also stood out, due to the unique construction techniques of the IDF. These included stone-filled gabions, long rectangular blockhouses and extensive use of pre-made metal positions for machine guns.

When someone thinks about undertaking looking for something the size of the Bar Lev Line, the mind briefly fills with romantic notions of battlefields left just the way they were after the battle. Time and other realities tend to dash these notions rather quickly. My search for the Bar Lev Line was no different. Most of the positions I found bore little resemblance to their original state. Further, the Egyptian Government has made significant efforts to 'clean' the Sinai of the wreckage of war. The following is what I found the conditions of the various positions to be during my searches:

Maoz Nisan: Buried by dredging.
Maoz Mafzeah: Currently within the confines of an Egyptian army unit. Unable to confirm if anything remains.
Maozim Zidon and Lituf: Utterly destroyed and highly dangerous, due to excessive UXOs (over 1,800 counted by me personally).
Maozim Botzer and Matzmed: Unable to find, believe buried as a result of dredging.
Taoz Hurva: Some remains of structures, but the area is currently used as an ammunition supply point (ASP) by the Egyptian army.
Maoz Purkan: Currently the site of Ferry Crossing 6 at Ismailiya. The area directly behind is an Egyptian army Training Camp.
Taoz Televizia: In the Egyptian Military Zone. Somewhat intact, but littered with exposed mines.
Maoz Hizayon: Mostly buried by dredging. Some small positions visible on the embankment.
Taozim Havraga and Maror: Unable to be found. The areas are now highly populated and cultivated.
Maoz Mifreket: Utterly destroyed. It can be seen while crossing the Mubarak Peace Bridge at Qantara.
Maozim Milano, Matzmed, Botzer, Ketuba, Drora, Lahtzanit and Orkal: Buried under dredging. Some twisted metal of Milano is still visible if driving along the east bank of the Suez Canal.
Maoz Budapest: Buried by time, or deliberately by the Egyptians. The area of the position has now been made into a container facility.
Taoz Traklin: Taken over by Egyptian army and used as an active base, complete with the surface laid minefield to the west of the position.
Taoz Notsa: 30:01.83N–32:41.04E. Abandoned. Two main bunkers that are accessible. Large fields of refuse, to include at least one MG. Numerous tank emplacements that have not been fully explored.
Taoz Tzeidar: 29:53.54N–32:38.10E. Currently a museum along the Sharm el Sheik Road. A tourist attraction run by a major and a squad of soldiers. LE5 entry fee. Guided tour by English speaking Egyptian Soldier. Formerly a 155mm battery position of the IDF. Five gun points destroyed, one still functional.
Taoz Nozel: 30:36.46N–32:23.49E. Currently a museum, but inaccessible to the public. Forward of the position are former trench lines of the Israeli Army, as well as three destroyed T-54 tanks. Two main bunkers, with an extensive amount of vehicles including tanks.

Maoz Masreq: 29:56.08N–32:34.14E. Across from Suez City. Blown up SU-76 nearby. Two bunkers blown professionally, lots of refuse. One bunker untouched, but surrounded by single strand and coiled concertina wire.

Maoz Lakekan: 30:23.81N–32:24.49E. Currently a museum, unavailable to the public, although well marked. One primary bunker. Two small out-buildings, that house a display of weapons and documents of the battle. The outside has a number of vehicles including tanks, jeeps and a 120mm mortar.

I was very fortunate to have served in the Sinai. The area that encompassed the Bar Lev Line is currently a closed Egyptian Military Area. Traffic is highly regulated and there are numerous checkpoints. The Egyptian Military and Police Forces were extremely kind in letting me carry out my duties as a UN Observer, while at the same time indulging in my historical hobby. The people of the Sinai, both Egyptian and Bedouin, were a constant source of information during my searches, and there was never a village where I and my teammates were not welcomed with open arms and warm hospitality.

BIBLIOGRAPHY

Aboul-Enein, Youssef, 'The Yom Kippur War: Memoirs Of Egyptian Generals' *Military Review* Jan–Feb 2003

Aloni, Shlomo, *Arab-Israeli Air Wars 1947–1982* Osprey Publishing, Oxford, 2000

Adan, Avraham, *On the Banks of the Suez* Arms and Armour Press, London, 1980

Bar-Siman-Tov, Yaacov, *The Israeli-Egyptian War of Attrition 1969–1970* Columbia University Press, New York, 1980

Bolia, Robert, 'Israel And The War Of Attrition' *Military Review* Mar–Apr 2004

Cohen, Chaim, 'Military Engineering In The Sinai Desert' *The Military Engineer* Nov–Dec 1973

Creveld, Martin Van, *The Sword And The Olive – A Critical History Of The Israeli Defense Force* Public Affairs, New York, 1998

Dunstan, Simon, *The Yom Kippur War – the Arab-Israeli War of 1973* Osprey Publishing, Oxford, 2007

Dupuy, Trevor, *Elusive Victory – The Arab-Israeli War 1947–1974* Macdonald and Janes, London, 1978

El-Rewany, Hassan Ahmed, *The Ramadan War: End Of Illusion* US Army War College, Carlisle Barracks, 2001

Gawrych, George, 'Israeli Defensive Measures Against Arab Artillery' *Combat Studies Institute Report No. 13 Tactical Responses To Concentrated Artillery* US Army Command and General Staff College, Fort Leavenworth, Kansas

Herzog, Chaim, *The Arab-Israeli Wars – War and Peace in the Middle East* Arms and Armour Press, London, 1982

Morris, Benny, *Righteous Victims – a History of the Zionist-Arab Conflict 1181–1999* Alfred A. Knopf, New York, 2000

Nordeen, Lon, 'Egypt In The War Of Attrition' *International Air Power Review*, Spring 2003

Nordeen, Lon, *Air Warfare In The Missile Age* Smithsonian Institution Press, Washington DC, 2002

Rabinovitch, Abraham, *The Yom Kippur War – the Epic Encounter That Transformed the Middle East* Schoken Books, New York, 2004

Zaloga, Steven, *Red Sam – The Sa-2 Guideline Anti-Aircraft Missile* Osprey, Oxford, 2007

GLOSSARY

AAA	anti-aircraft artillery
AFB	air force base
AFV	armoured fighting vehicle
APC	armoured personnel carrier
ATGW	anti-tank guided weapon
EAF	Egyptian Air Force
GOC	general officer commanding
IAC	Israeli Armored Corps
IAF	Israeli Air Force
IDF	Israel Defense Forces
INS	Israel Navy Ship
MBT	main battle tank
NATO	North Atlantic Treaty Organisation
RPG	rocket-propelled grenade
SAM	surface-to-air missile
SEAL	sea air land Special Forces
SPG	self-propelled gun
TAP	Trans-Arabian Pipeline
UN	United Nations
UNTSO	United Nations Truce Supervisory Organisation

INDEX